NOIR
the art of Rob Moran

AIRSHIP 27 PRODUCTIONS

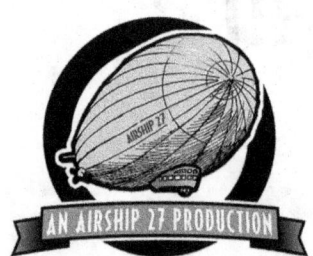

Noir: The Art of Rob Moran
© 2014 Rob Moran

This book is dedicated to my biggest fan, best friend and the love of my life…my wife, Aileen.
--Rob Moran

Published by Airship 27 Productions
www.airship27.com
www.airship27hangar.com

Cover and interior illustrations © 2014 Rob Moran

Editor: Ron Fortier
Production and design by Rob Davis.

ISBN-13: 978-0615988337
ISBN-10: 0615988334

Printed in the United States of America

10 9 8 7 6 5 4 3 2 1

NOIR
the art of Rob Moran

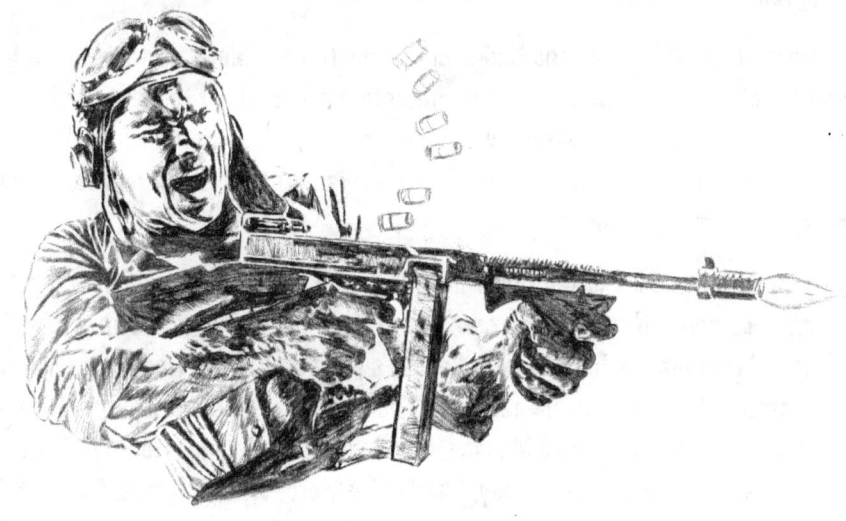

noir   [nwär]   **noun**
Noir is French for black and is a type of fiction or a film that has tough characters and is cynical, bleak and pessimistic in nature.

BLACK & WHITE

During the decade of the 1930s and 40s, American cinema produced some of the most brutal, intense crime/gangster films ever unleashed on the movie going public. Why this occurred I really couldn't tell you, I'm a movie buff, not a trained sociologist. But this is what I do know, starting with the 30s, studios like Warner Brothers began creating such memorable melodramas as *The Big House, Little Ceasar, The Public Enemy, Beast of the City, Scarface, Limehouse Blues, G-Men, The Petrified Forest* and *Angels With Dirty Faces.*

It seemed like over night such actors as James Cagney, Pat O'Brien, Edward G. Robinson, Joan Blondell, Jean Harlow, Walter Huston, Paul Muni, Claire Trevor, George Raft, Betty Davis, Spencer Tracy, Lloyd Nolan, Peter Lorre, Sydney Greenstreet, John Garfield and Humphrey Bogart had become Hollywood superstars by portraying either villainous mobsters or their rivals; the dedicated coppers. Most of these 30s offerings were tough-edged tales with gun-blasting shoot-outs in every other scene leading to the bloody demise of the crime boss in the final reel.

By the advent of the 40s, the tone had become much more bleak as the stories began to turn inward exploring the hopelessness of characters predestined to meet tragic fates. The brand *film noir,* French for black-film, was slapped on this new breed of fatalistic dramas. It was derived from the low-key black and white visual style which had its roots in the German Expressionist movement.

This new crop of hardboiled crime flicks included such greats as *High Sierra, This Gun for Hire, Double Indemnity, Crime,Inc., Detour, The Killers, Kiss of Death, Out of the Past, the Naked City*—all culminating in 1949 with Cagney's powerful *White Heat.* Among new tough guys and women added to the role call were such notables as Alan Ladd, William Bendix, Veronica Lake, Tom Neal, Raymond Massey, Ann Savage, Burt Lancaster, Ava Gardner, Lana Turner, Joan Crawford, Lawrence Tierney, Charles Bickford, Victor Mature, Robert Mitchum, Susan Hayward, Orson Wells, Rita Hayward and Kirk Douglas; just to name a handful who appeared on that giant silver screen in glorious black and white.

And therein lies the magic of those crime epics, they were revealed to us in the stark simplicity of opposite hues with no color to confuse their moral issues. Black and white, good and evil...and all the shades of gray that existed in between. That subtle gray of a thick fog over a city bridge broken by the footfalls of running feet and then a gunshot rings out and a body falls into the cold, deep river below.

Lost souls struggling for salvation against a cruel, almost sadistic fate that they had no chance of surviving. It was truly heady stuff and entertained millions during those aforementioned decades. Later when the filmmakers started adding garish color splashes to these crime thrillers that elusive atmosphere of the old potboilers seemed to evaporate right before our eyes. Somehow the stark reality of black and white refused to be captured even by the most sophisticated new coloring processes. But progress forever marches onward and there was nothing to be done for it. Movies would go to full color and *film noir* became a lost art to be shown only in art-houses, late night cable channels and lectured about in film schools. It was a bygone magic we could never hope to recapture.

At least not on film. But on paper, well that's a whole different story and one that is as amazing as the history of *film noir*. You see, during the heyday of those great silver screen crime plays, American magazines were lavishly adorned by brilliant illustrators who month after month filled their pages with breathtaking artwork. Alas, that old nemesis of craftsmanship, progress, would also rear its ugly head in this venue until by the 1960s most magazines were using photographs carefully airbrushed and then later manipulated computer imagery to run alongside their articles. Like the black and white era of films, the day of the illustrator had also come and gone.

Having been a lifelong fan of both these creative sensibilities, you can easily imagine my total shock and disbelief when, just a little over a year ago, I stumbled upon illustration art on the internet that quite brilliantly captured all the mood and mystery of those early crime movies. From that first illustration, I instantly recognized the actors with their .45 automatics blasting at unseen rivals off-page. There were the trenchcoats, the wide brimmed fedoras pulled down over their eyes, the dark alleys and the Tommy-gun wielding thugs. Never mind the slinky femme fatales stretched across the compositions in alluring poses that held the same sinful temptation once ignited by the likes of Turner and Bacall.

I was stunned, dazed, delighted. And then there was the artist's name, Rob Moran. I immediately sought out his webpage only to find more of his *film noir* pieces and was not disappointed. It didn't take the deductive powers of a Sherlock Holmes to recognize both a true artistic talent and bona fide connoisseur of those old gangster flicks in this one soul. Rob is that wonder of wonders, an artist who by some miracle, instinctively knows his subject matter and recreates it through both the power of his pencils and inks while at the same time infusing his art with the same gut-wrenching emotion that inspired those classic movie melodramas.

That he is a one-of-kind artist goes without saying. His popularity, via the internet, has grown in leaps and bounds as his work continues to pay homage to an era in film history so many of us love dearly. With each new image, he takes us back to those simpler times and shares with all of us a combination of beauty and brutality that was the hallmark of *film noir*. Collections such as the one you hold in your hands will continue to cement his place in today's artistic community proving him to be a truly unique visionary who just happen to cast his glance back at the past instead of the future.

We are all so damn glad he did.

Ron Fortier
Writer/Editor
11/5/2012
Fort Collins, CO.

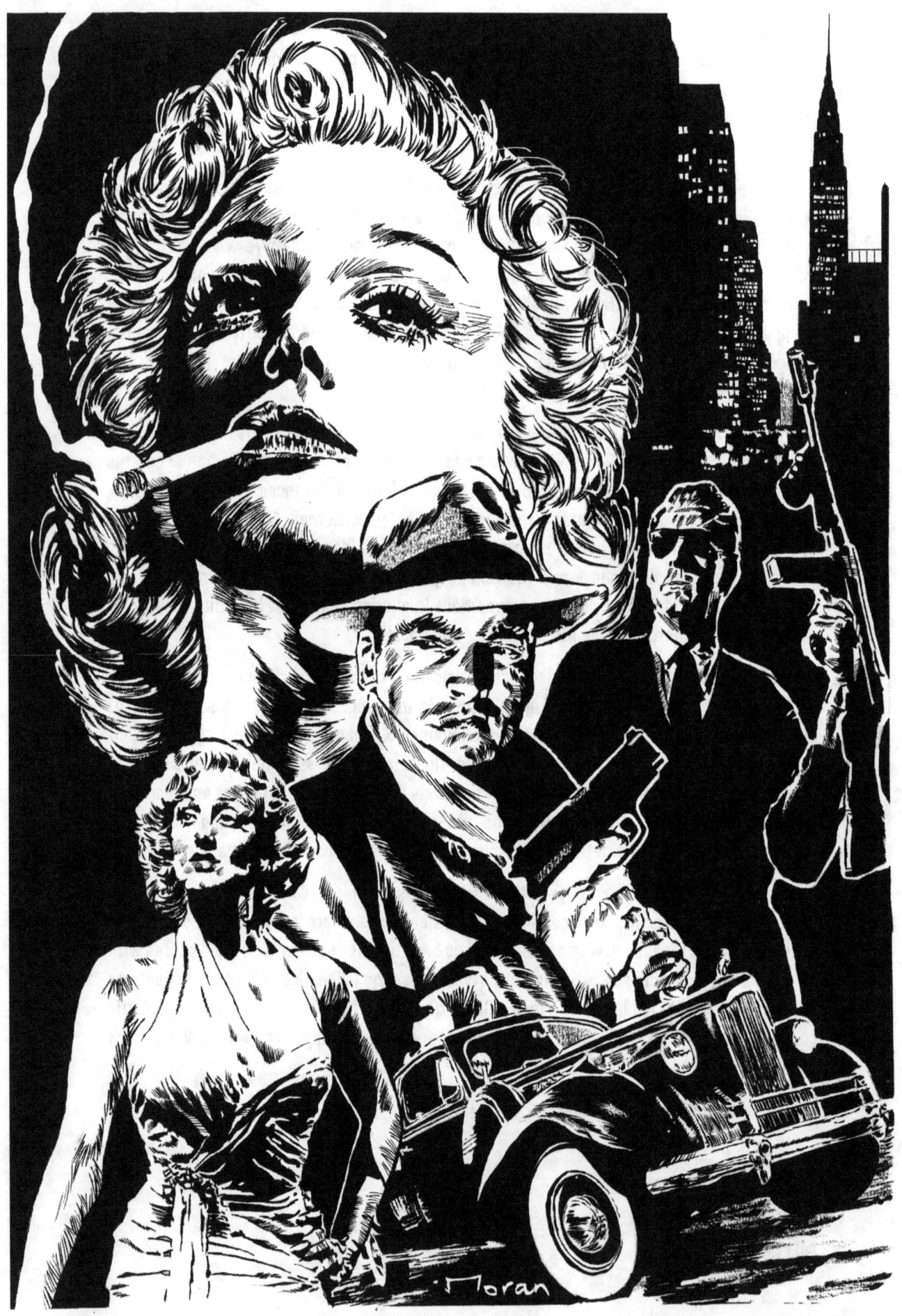

GALS, GUNS AND GANGSTERS

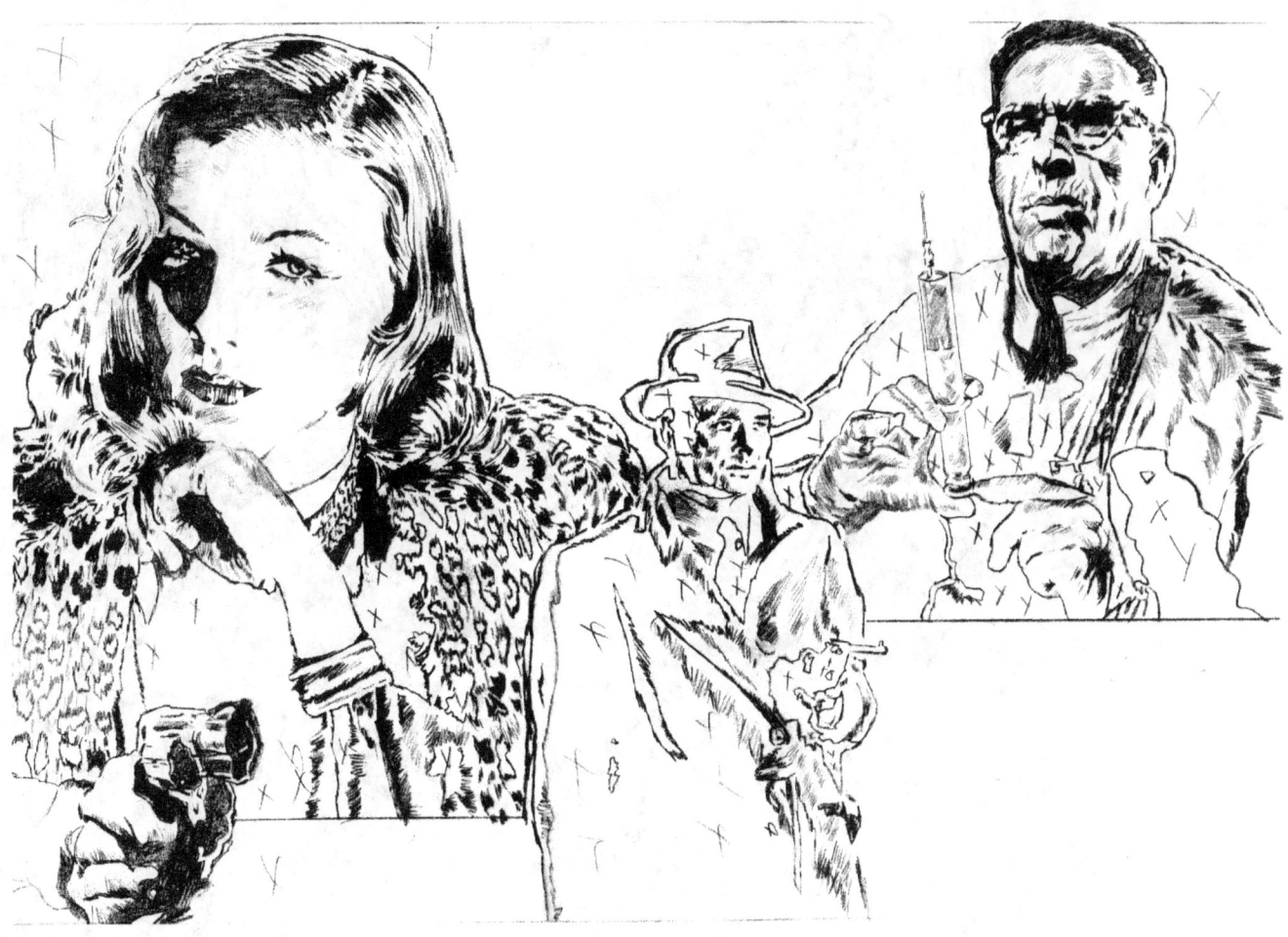

"I love NOIR ... the movies, the novels, the comic books; give me a story with sardonic guys and tough gals soaked in sleaze and shadows and I'm in Seventh Heaven."   — RM

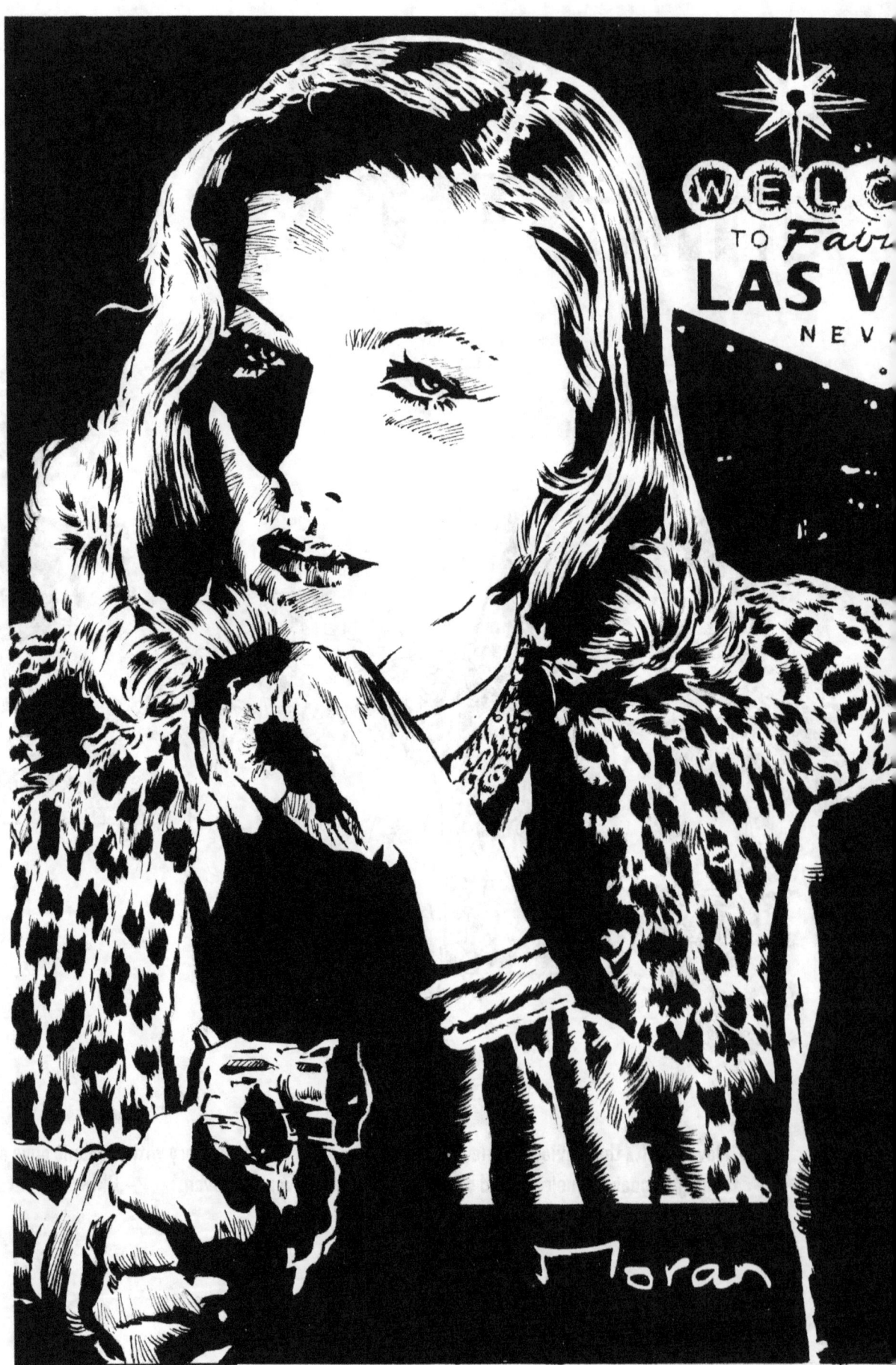

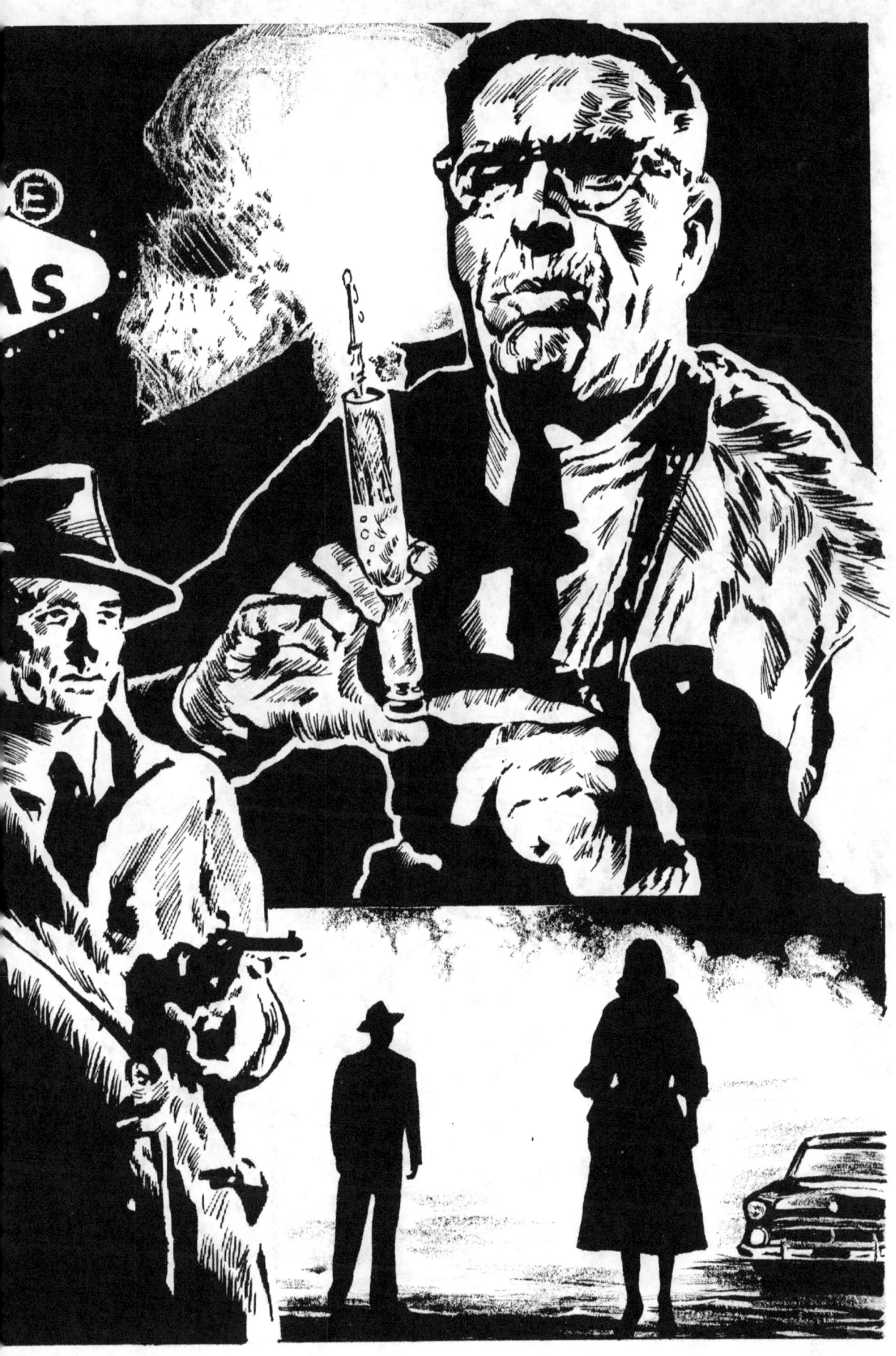

9

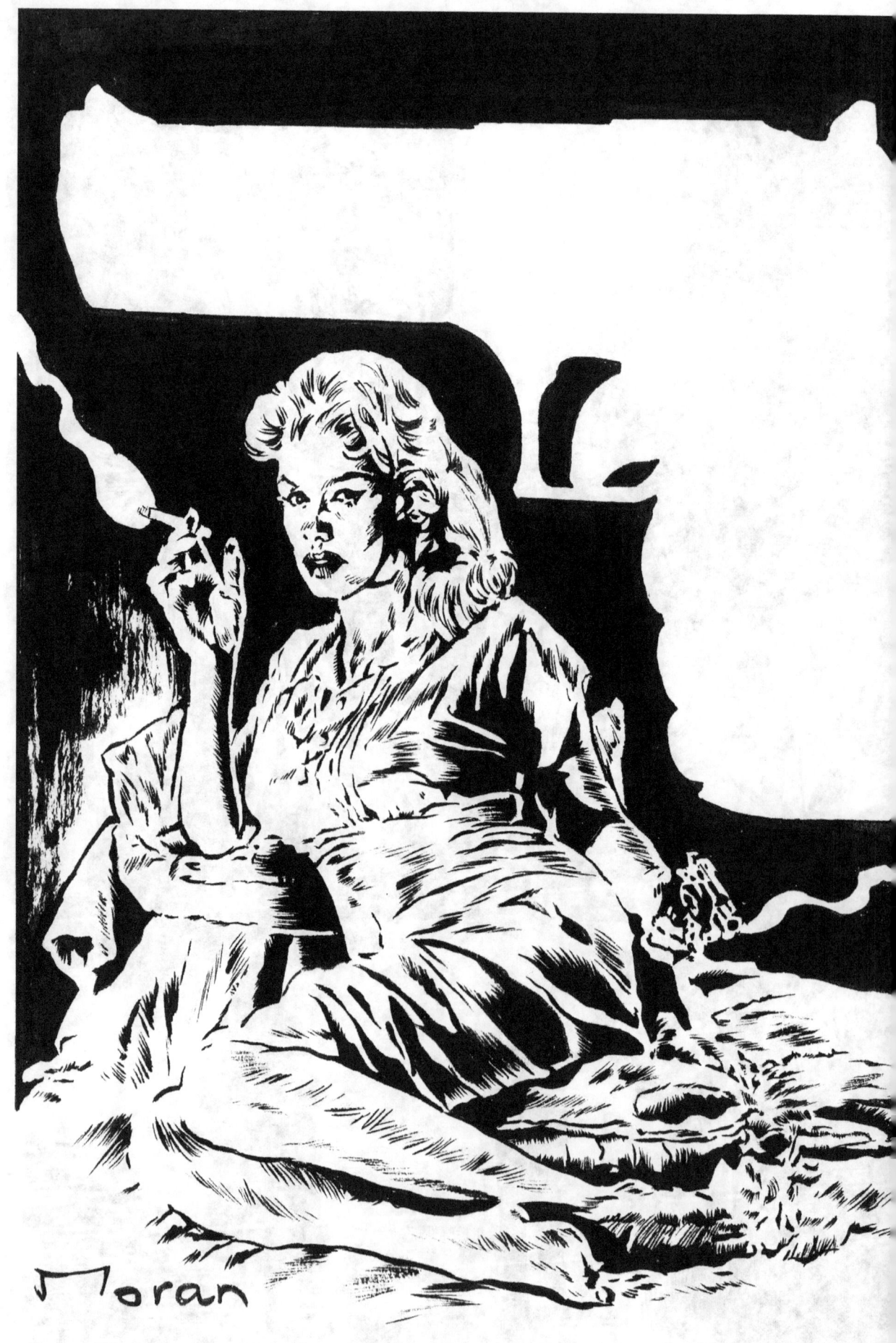

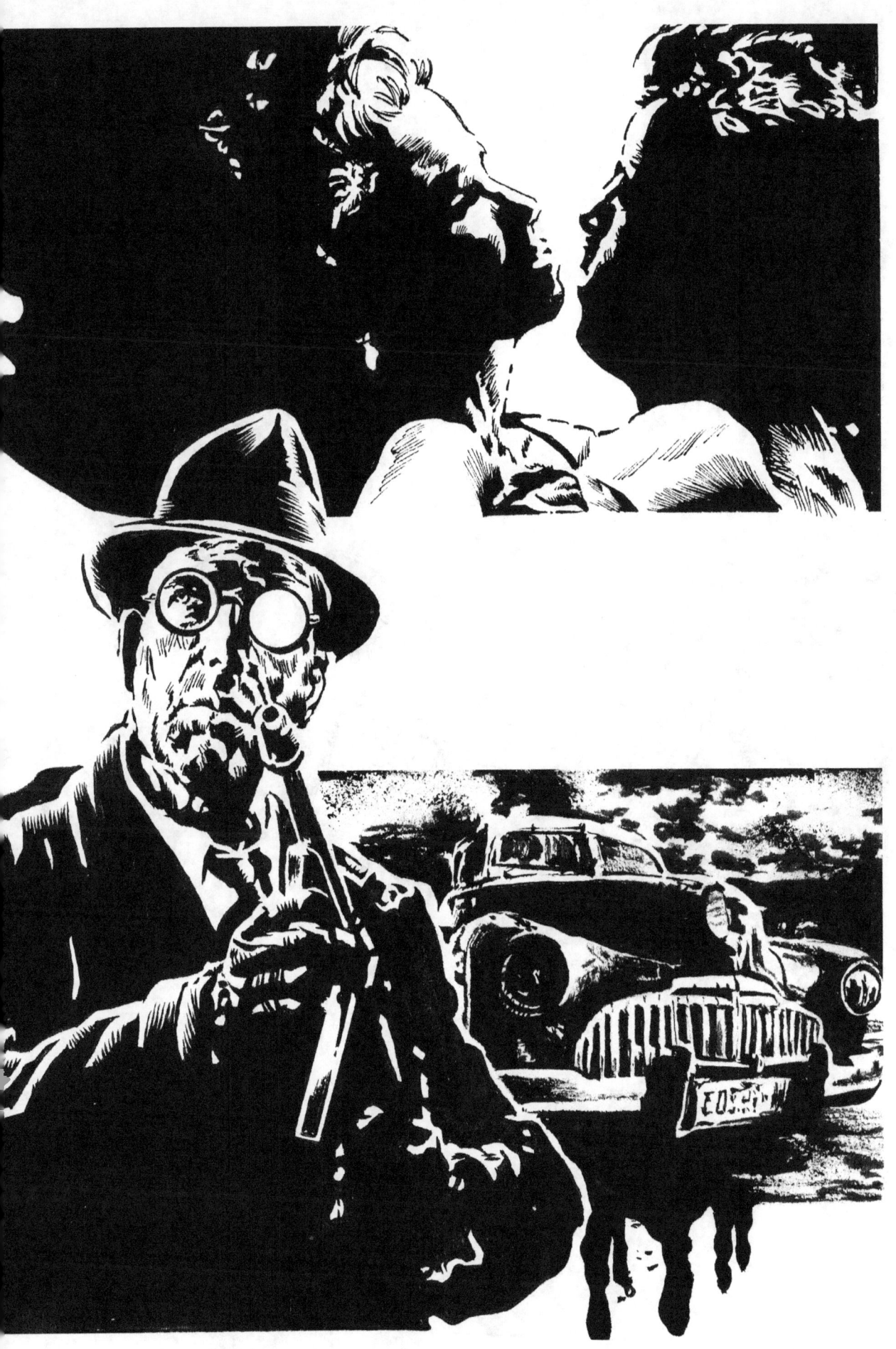

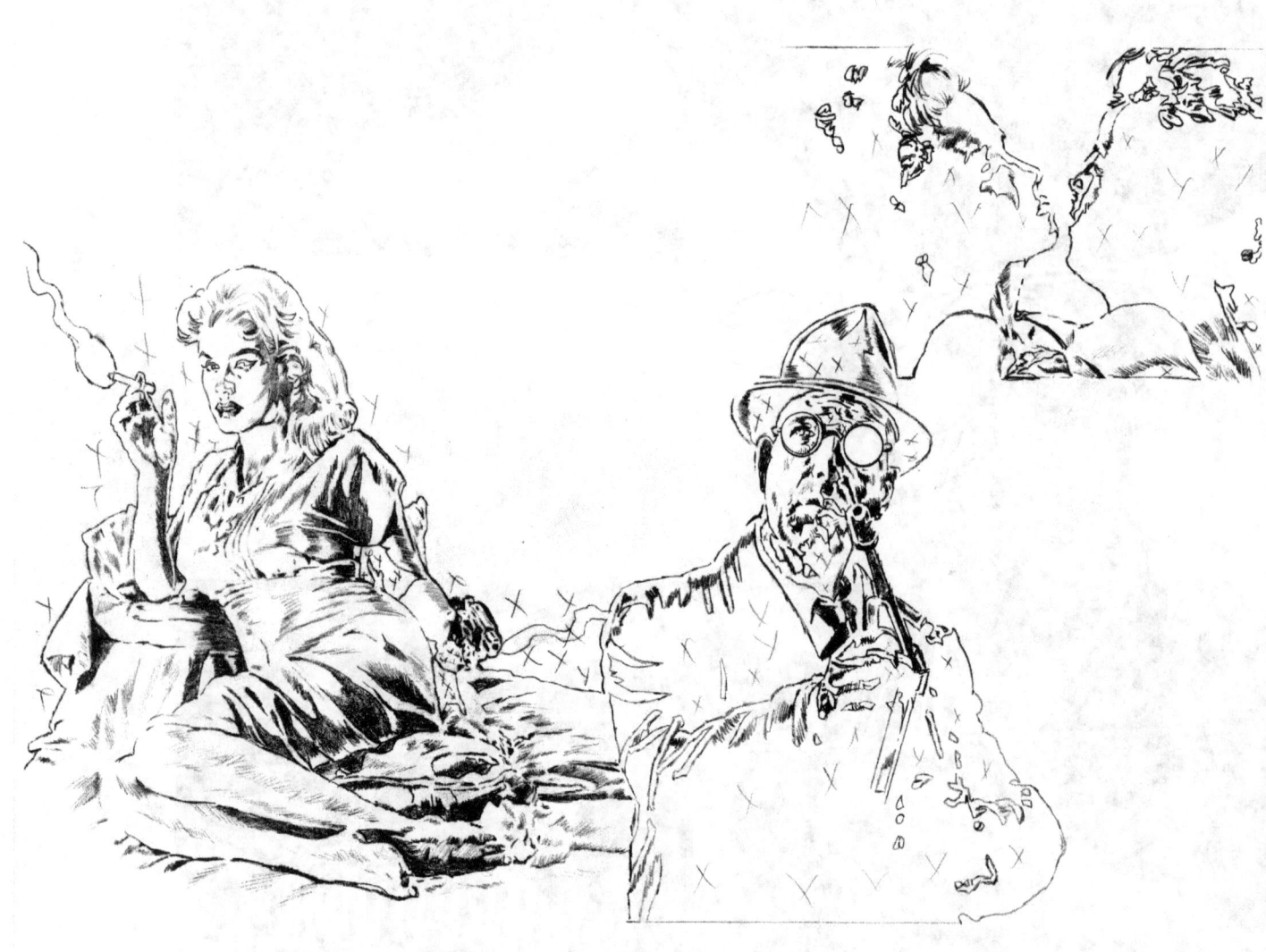

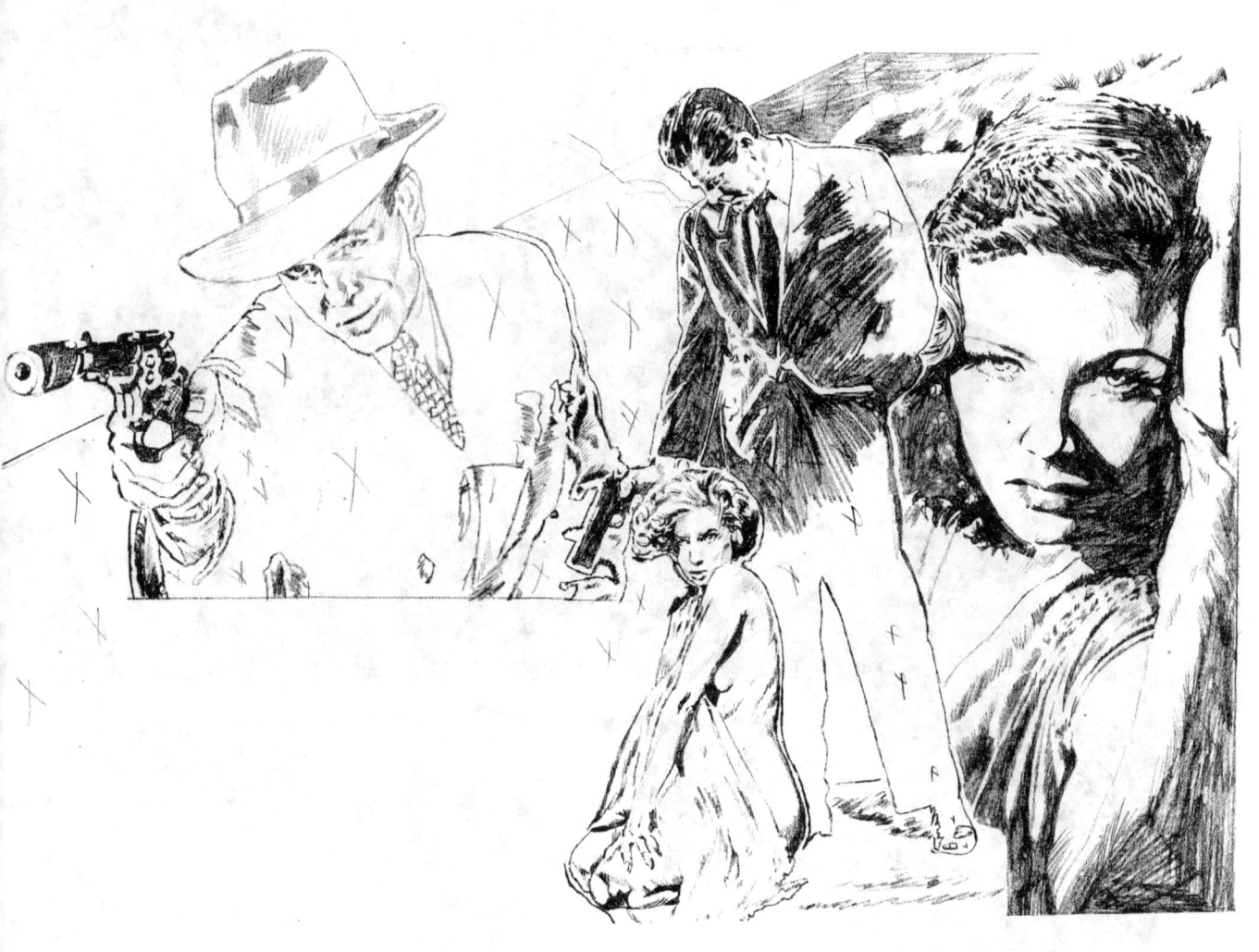

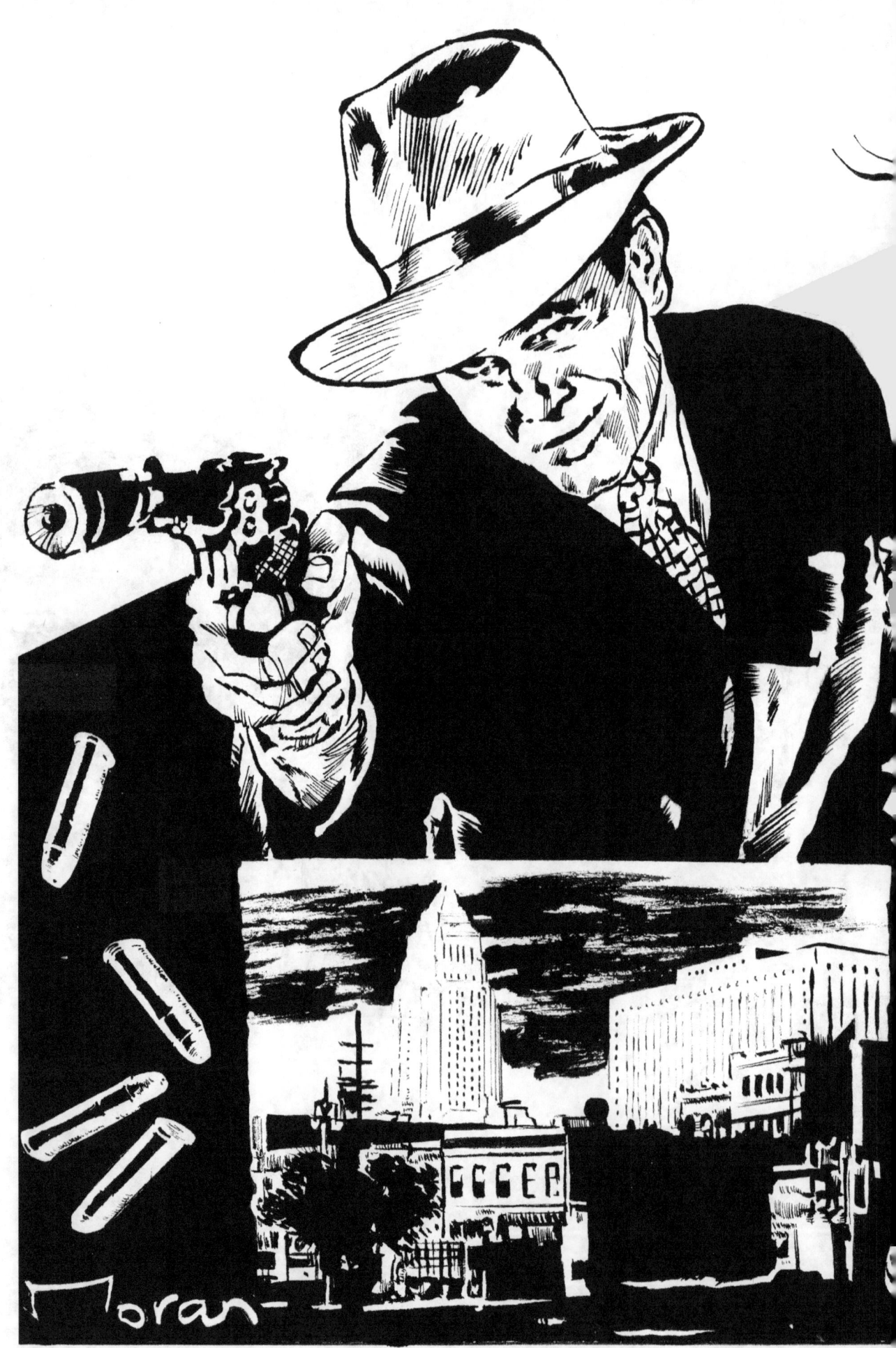

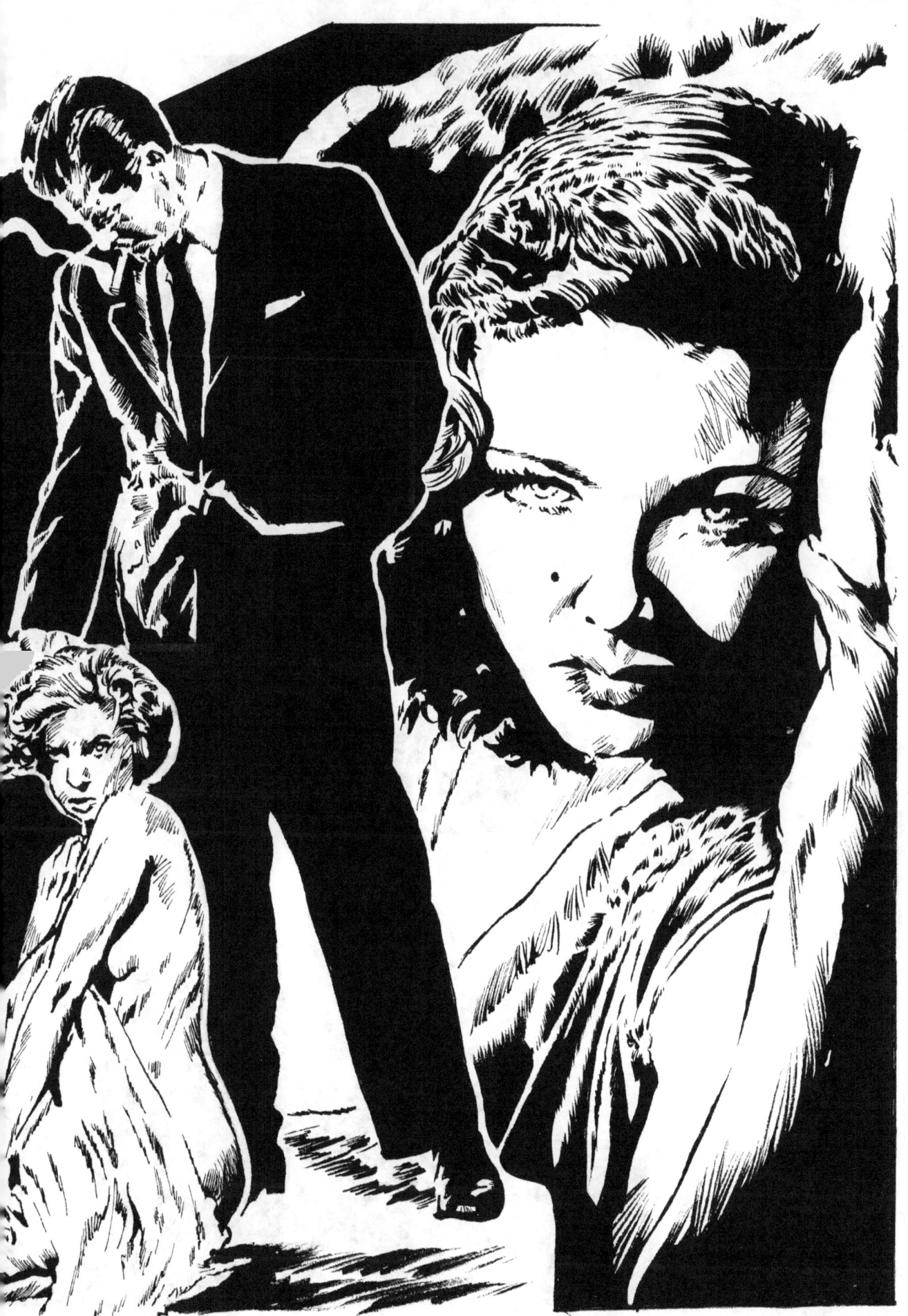

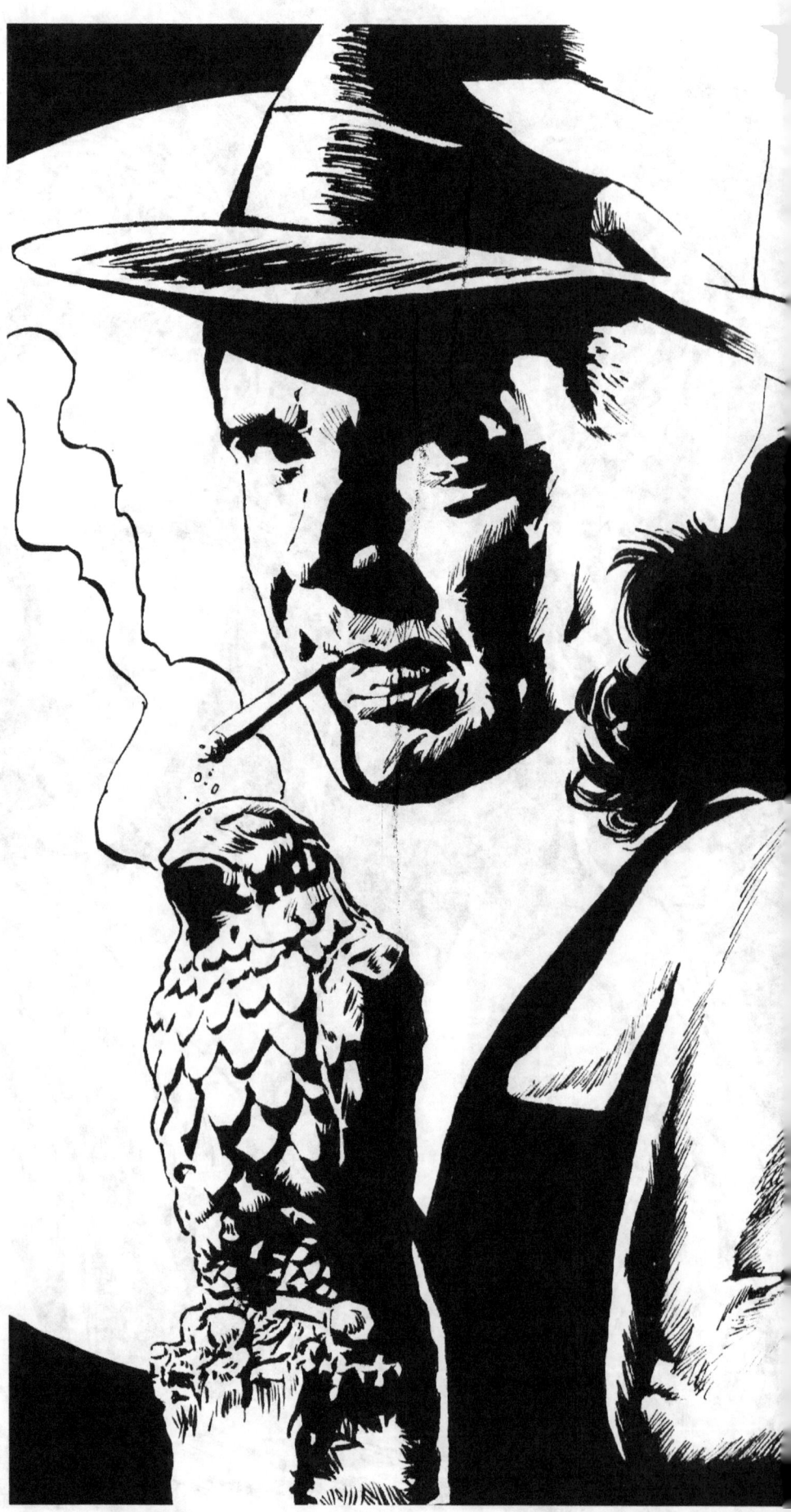

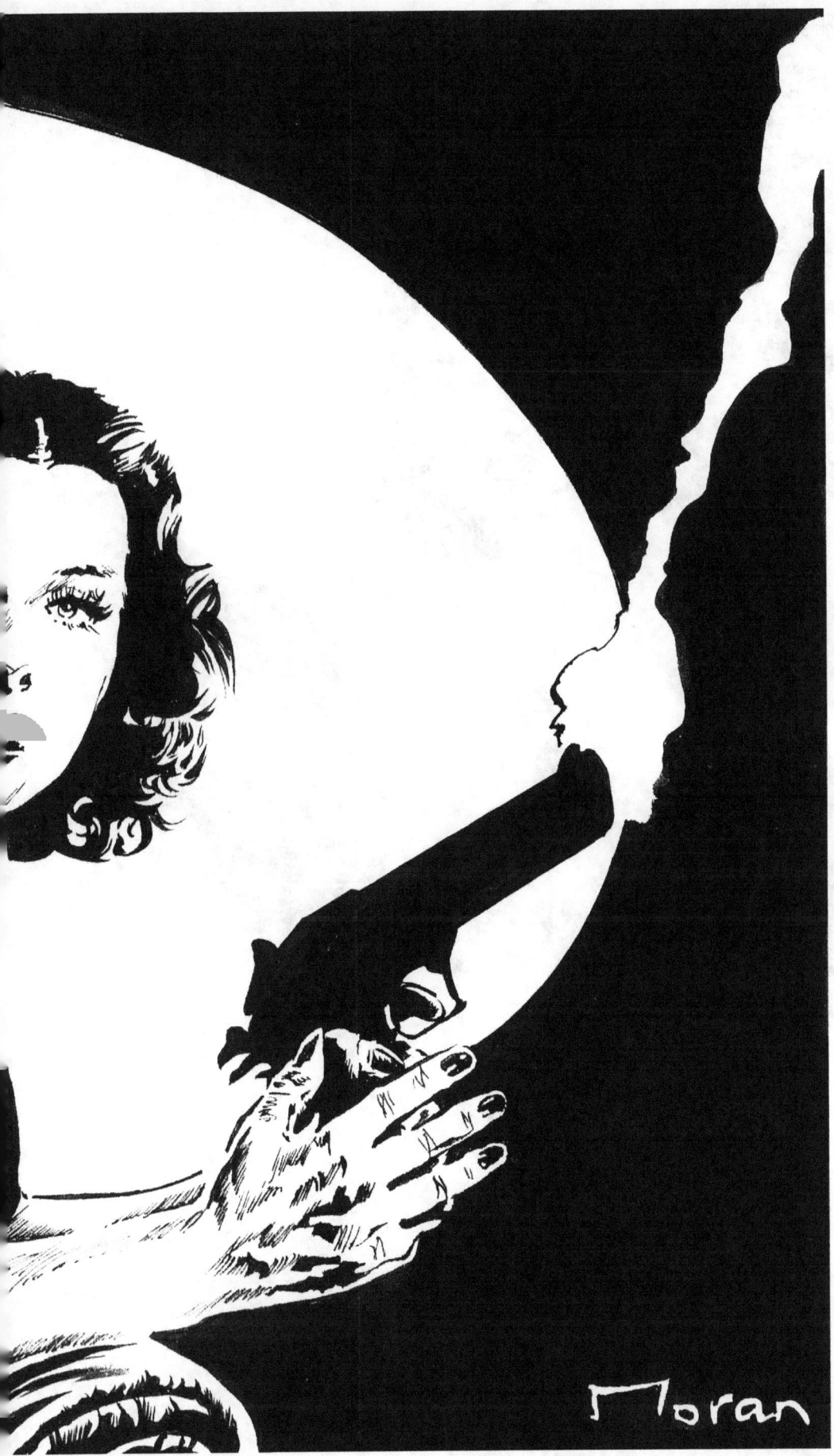

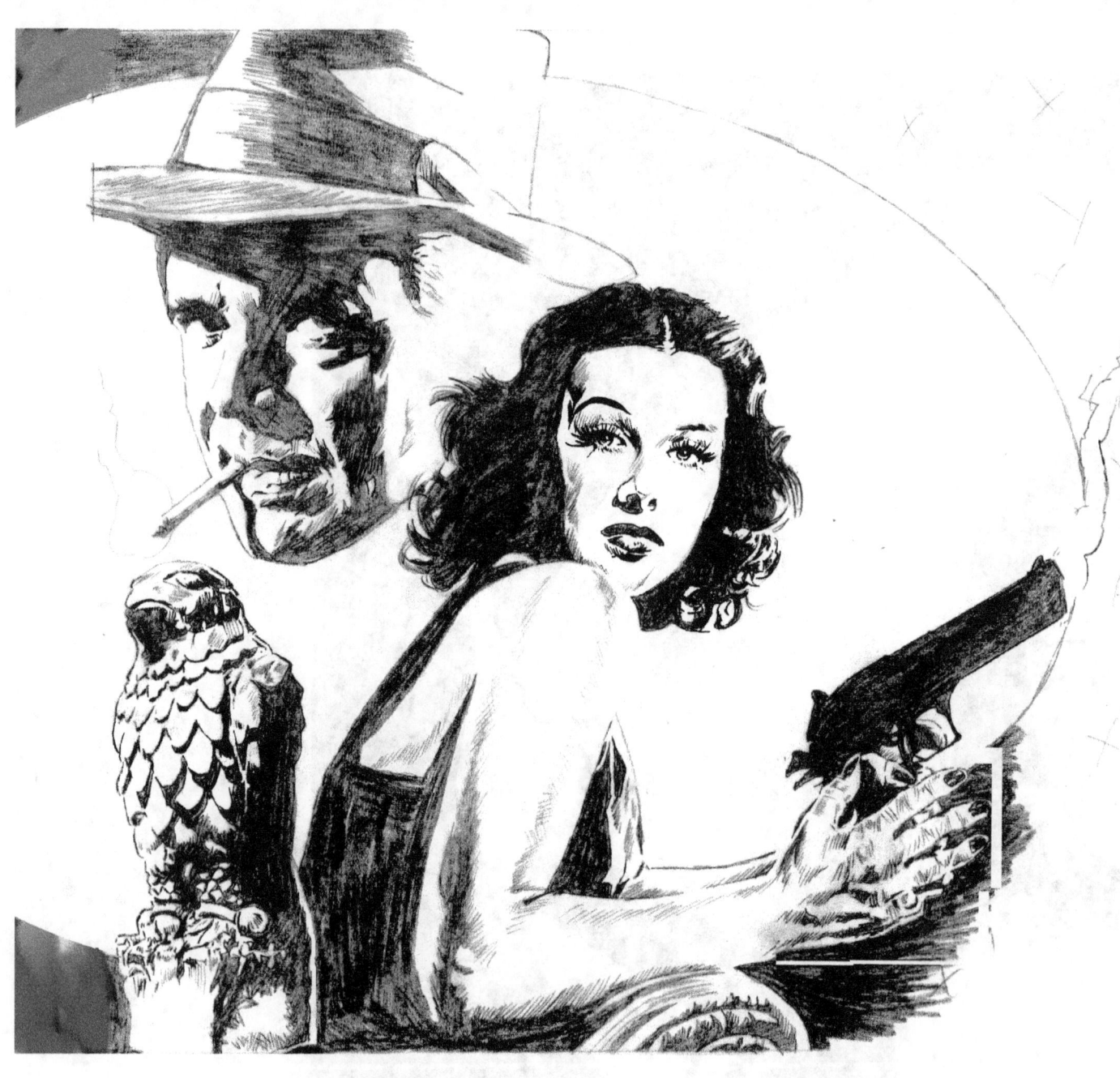

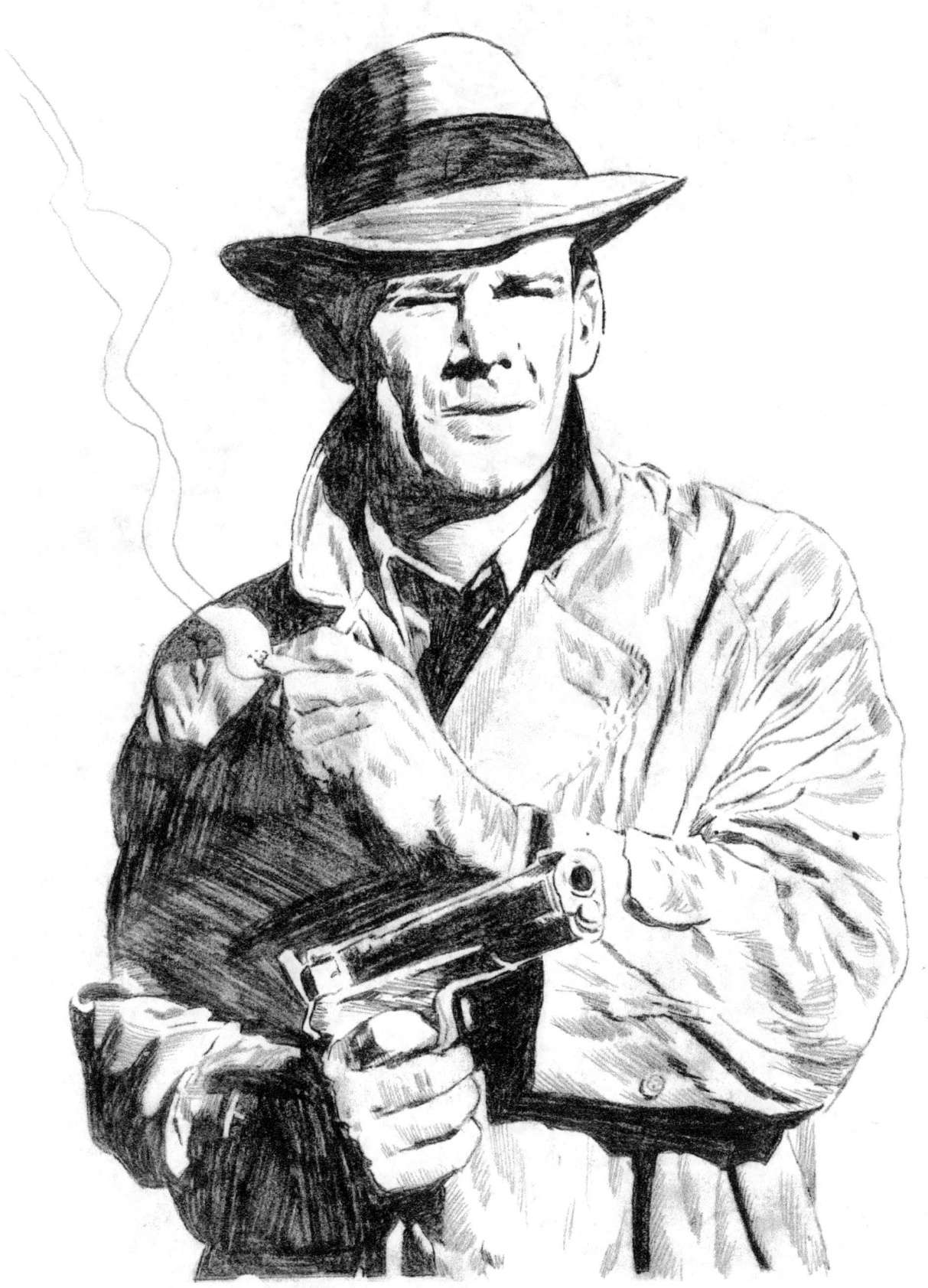

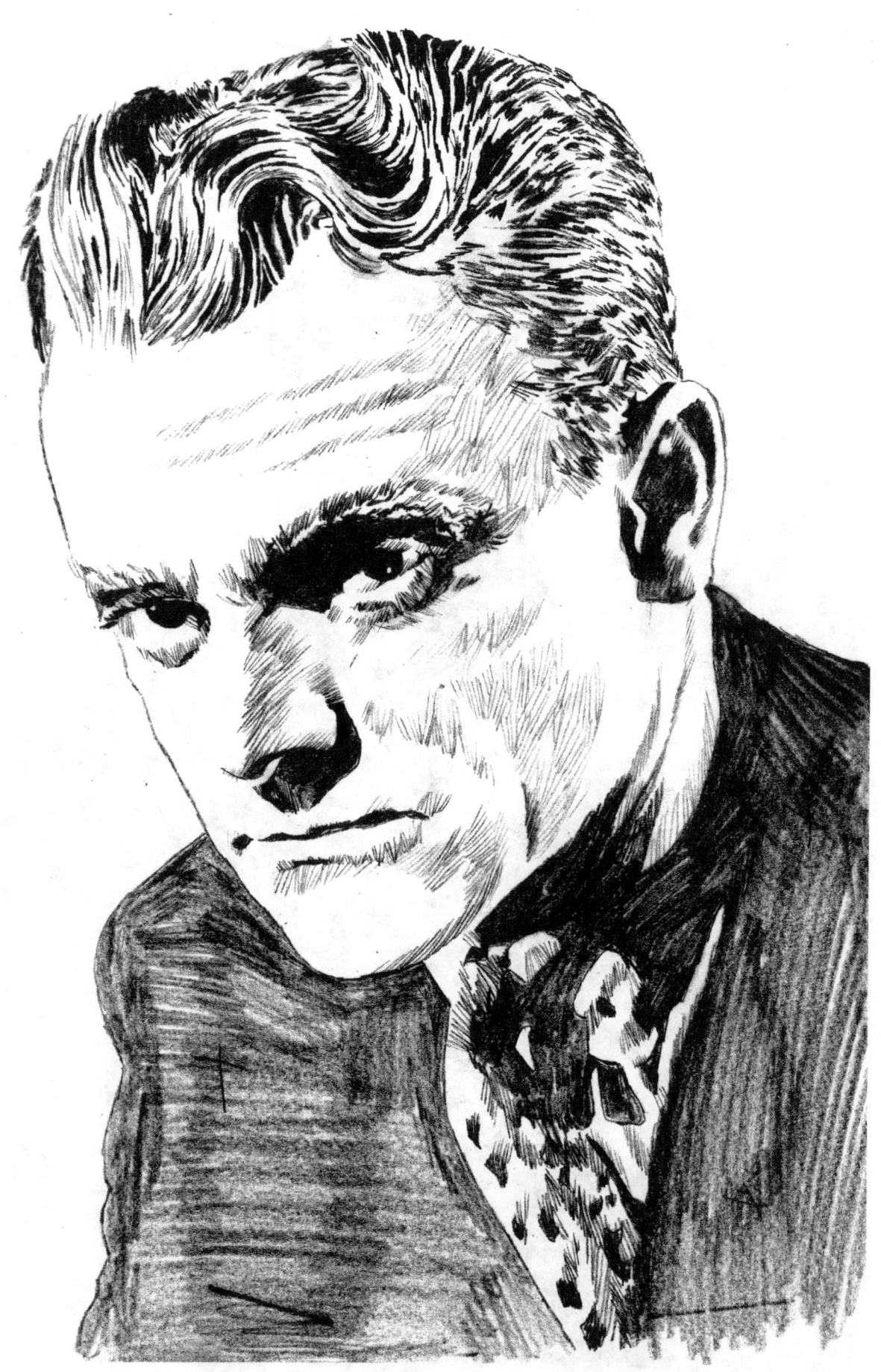

20

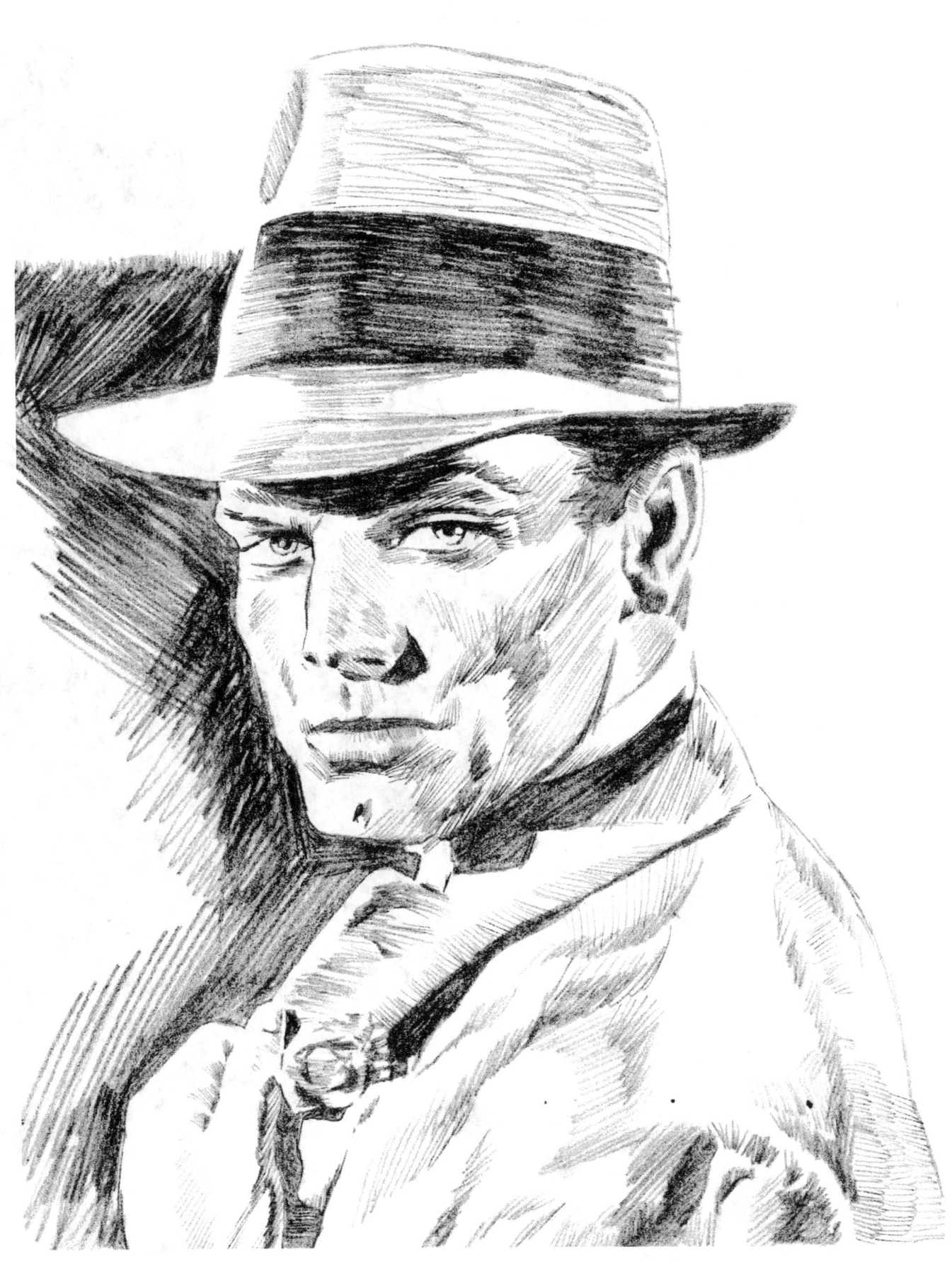

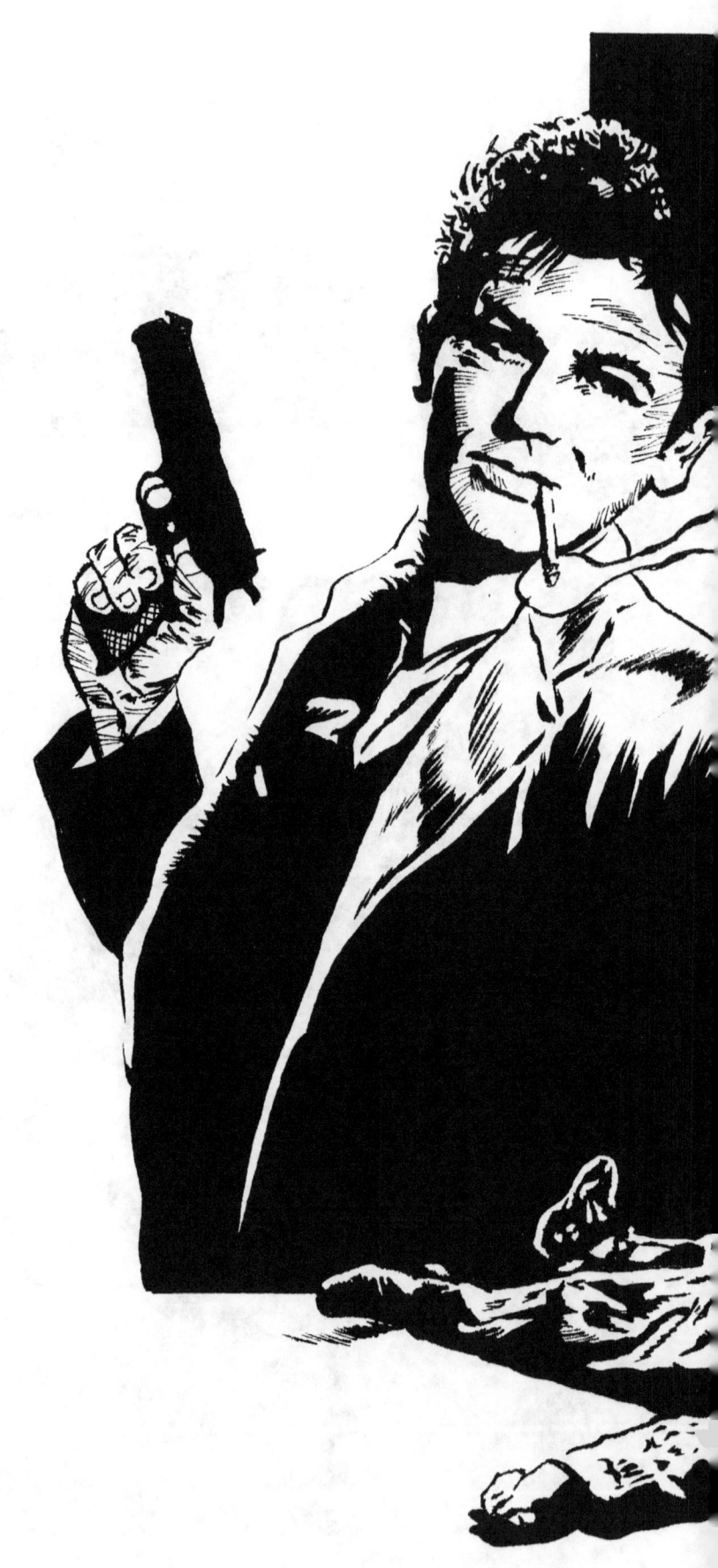

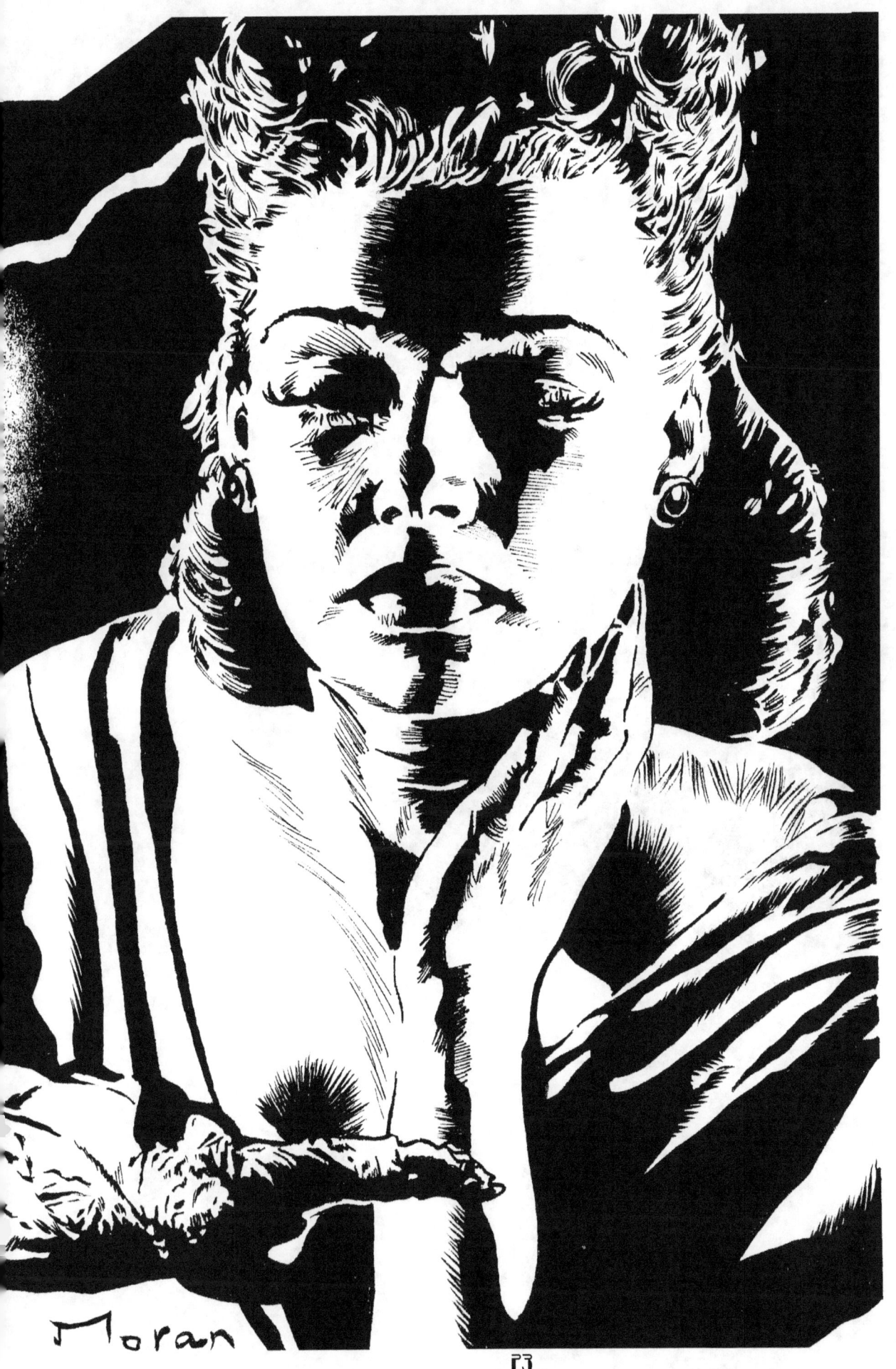

Moran

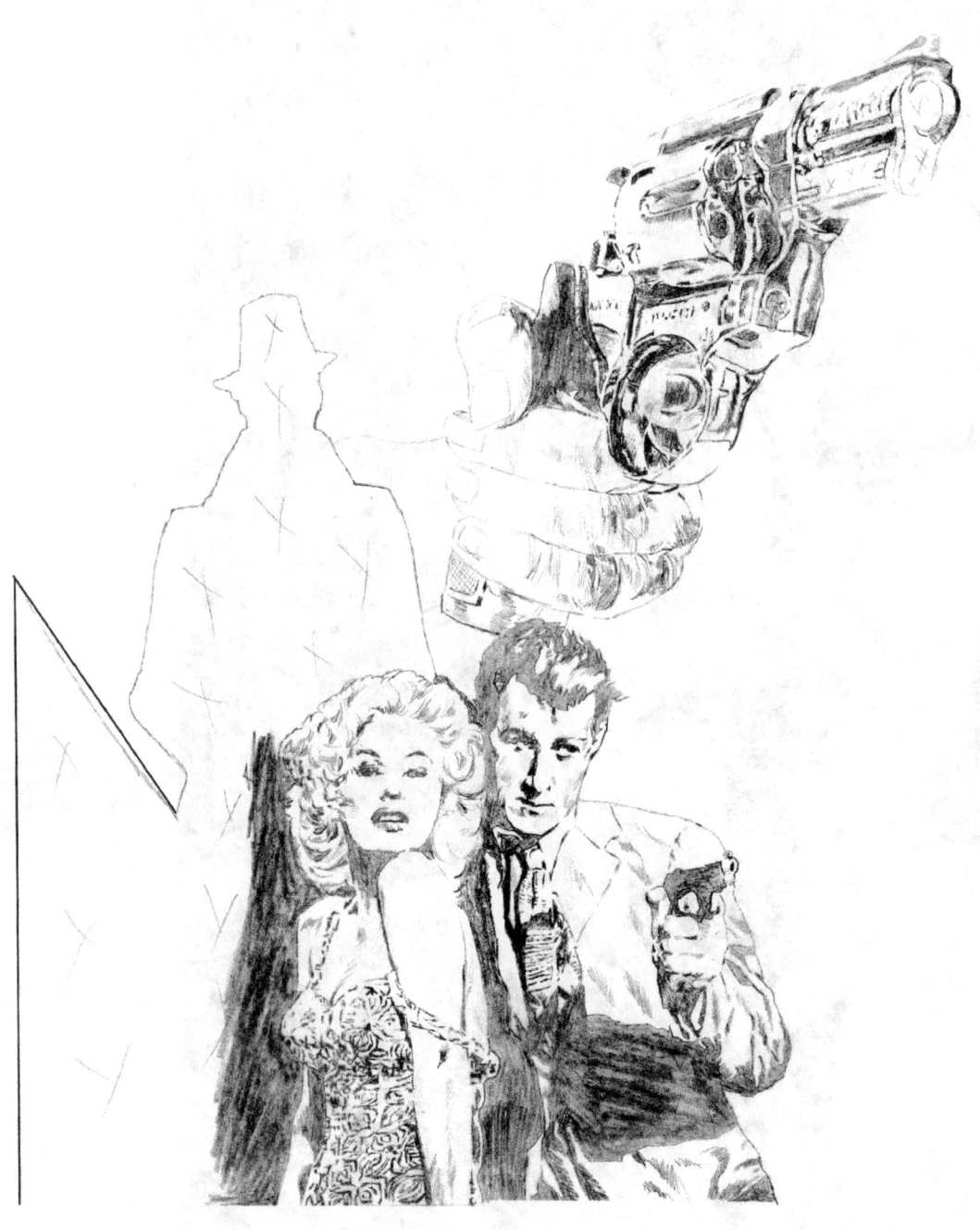

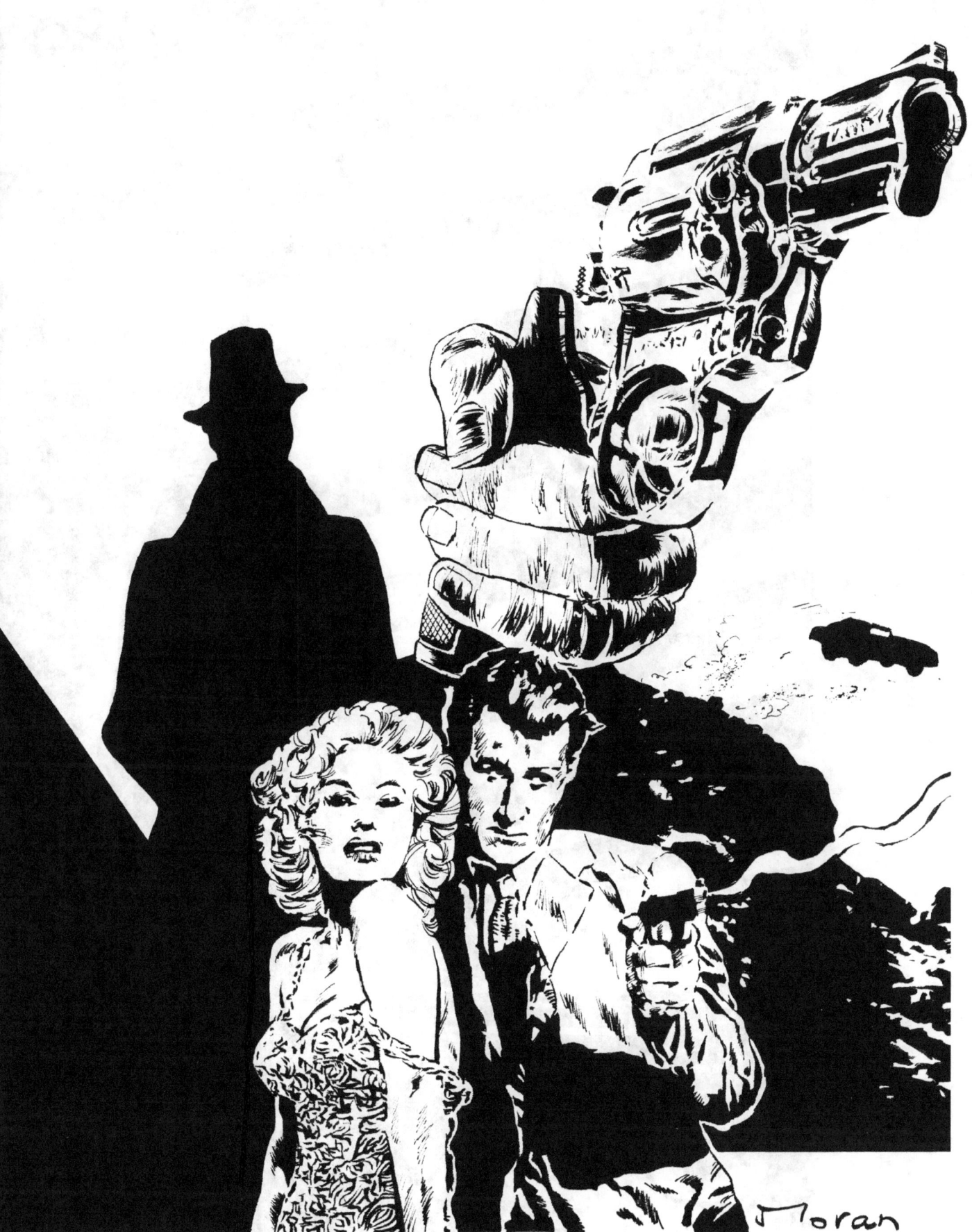

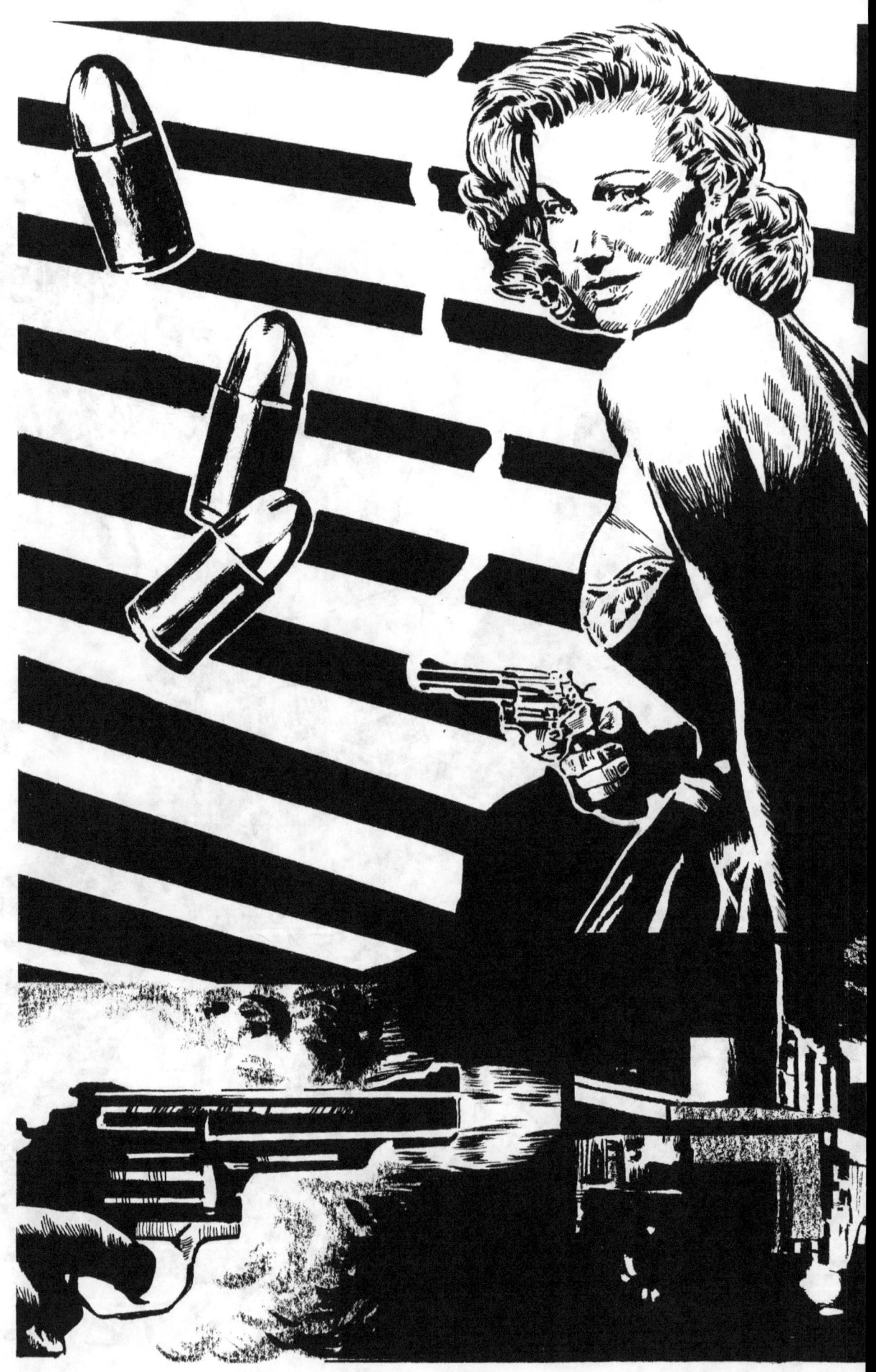

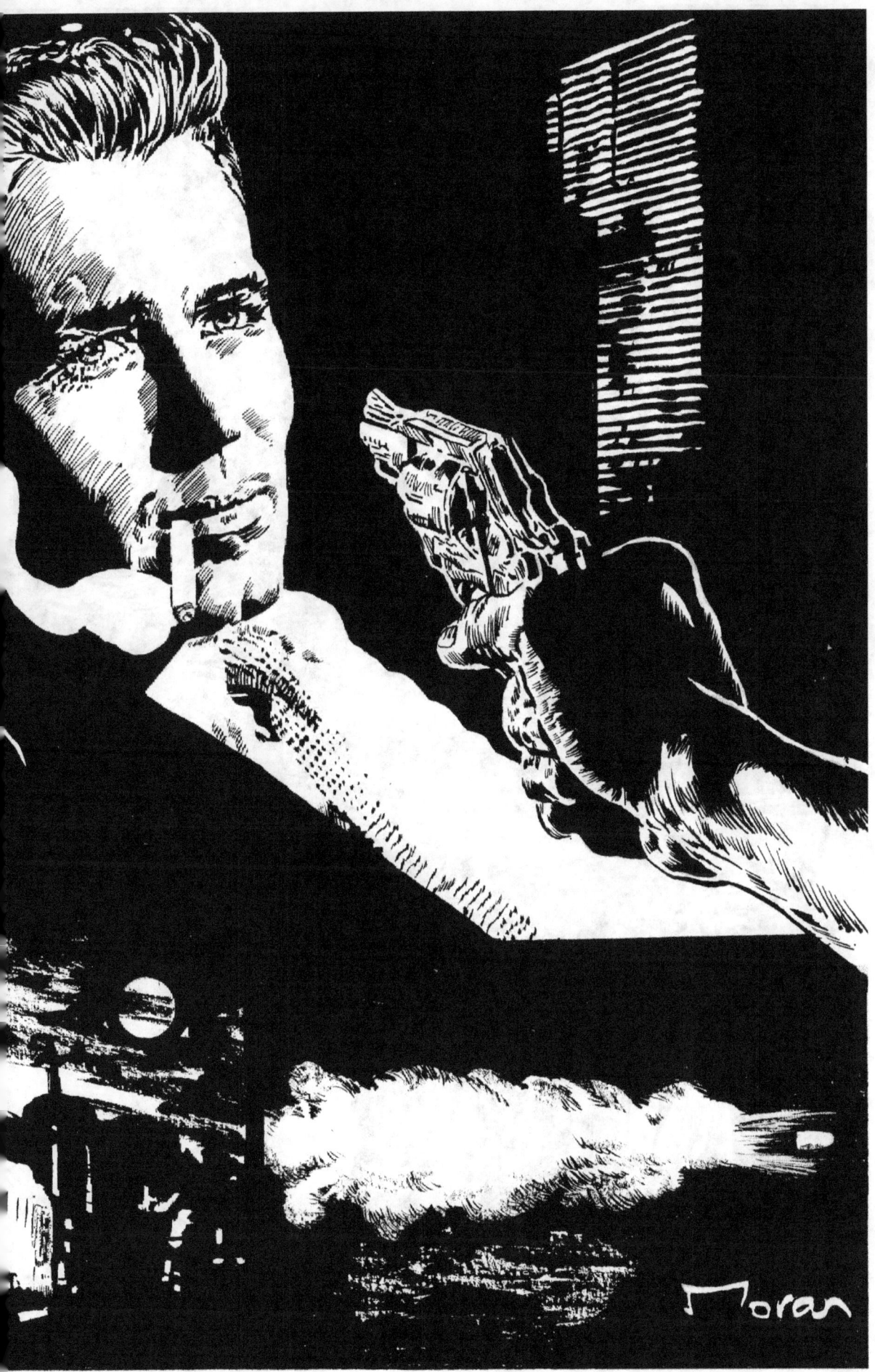

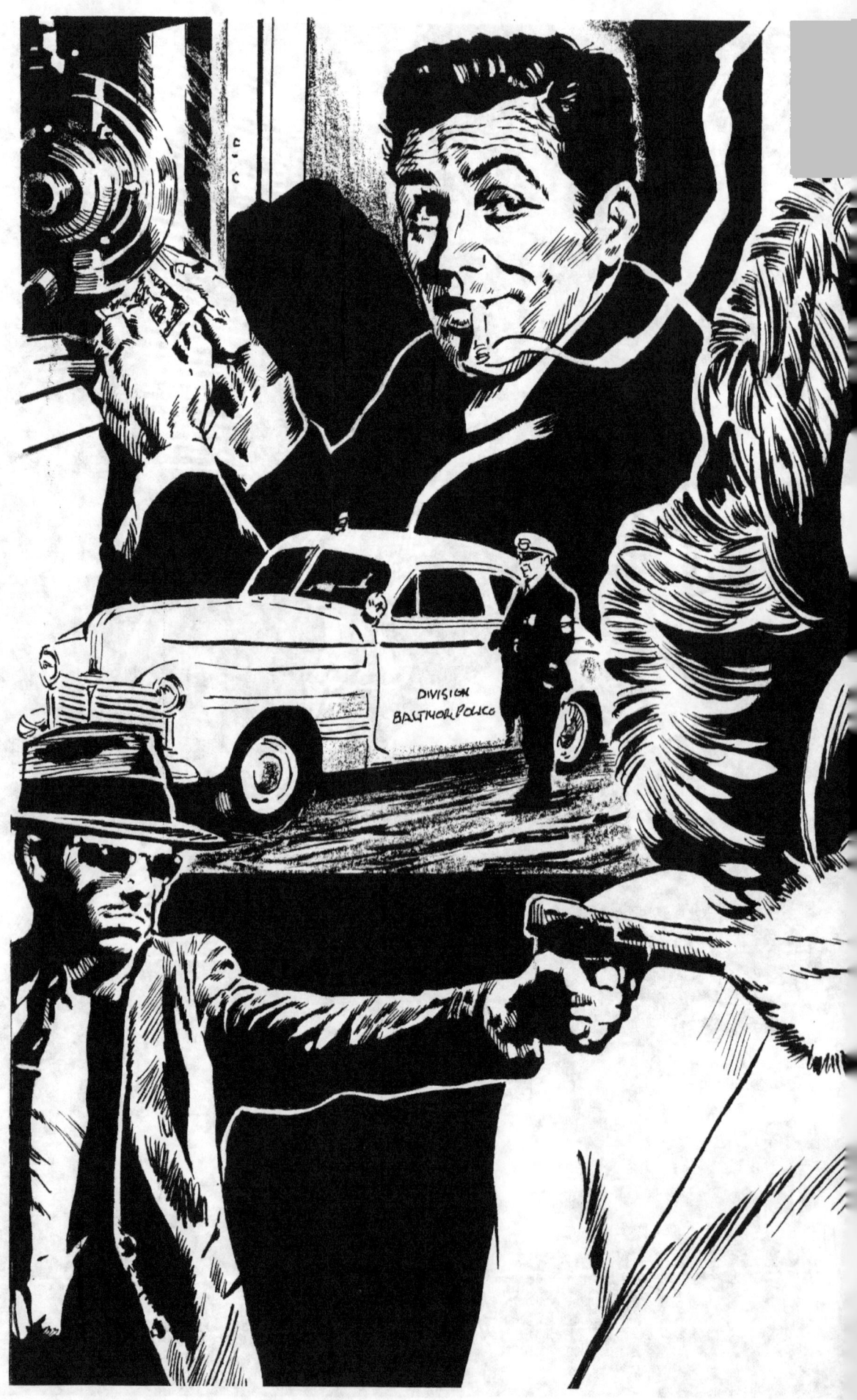

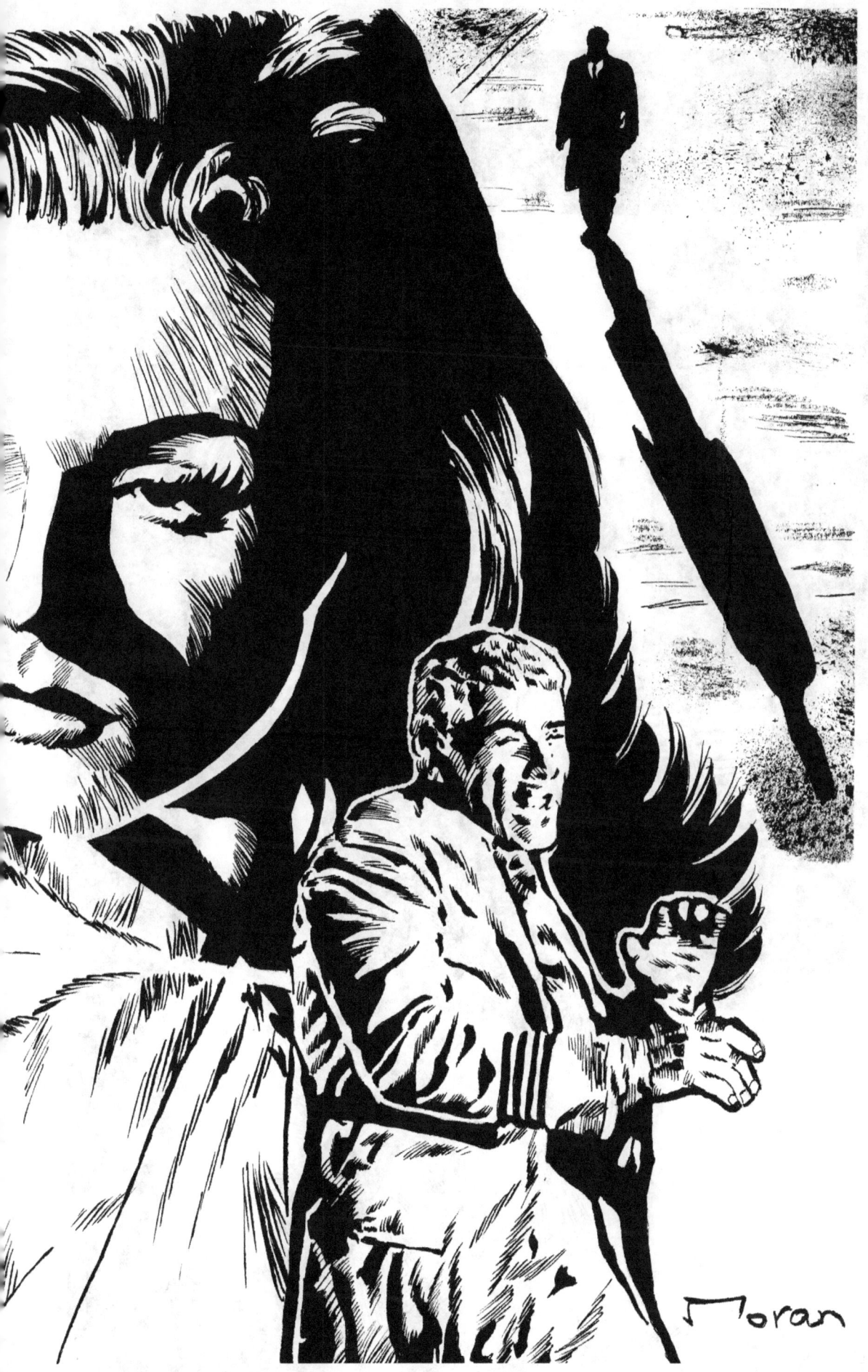

Moran

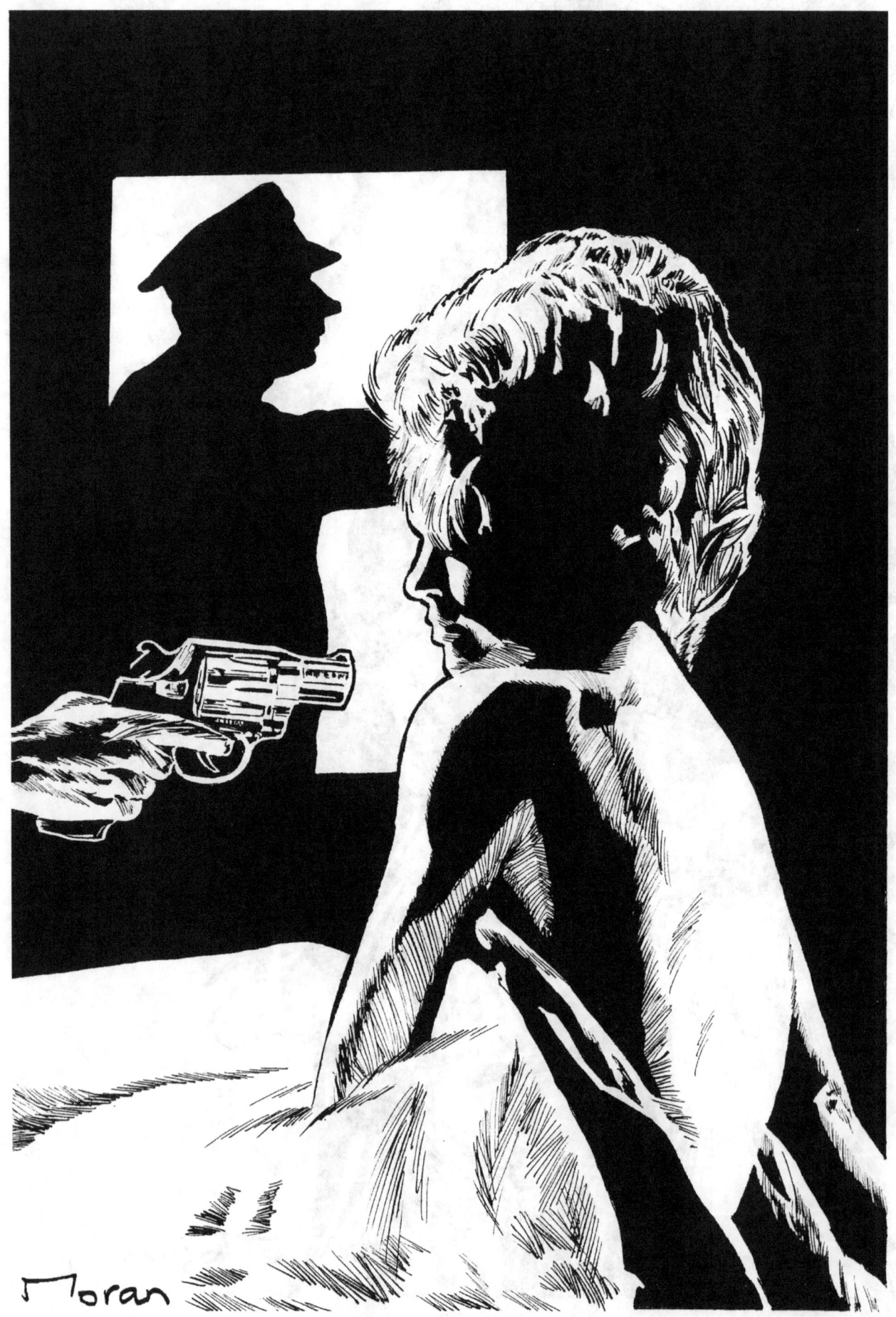

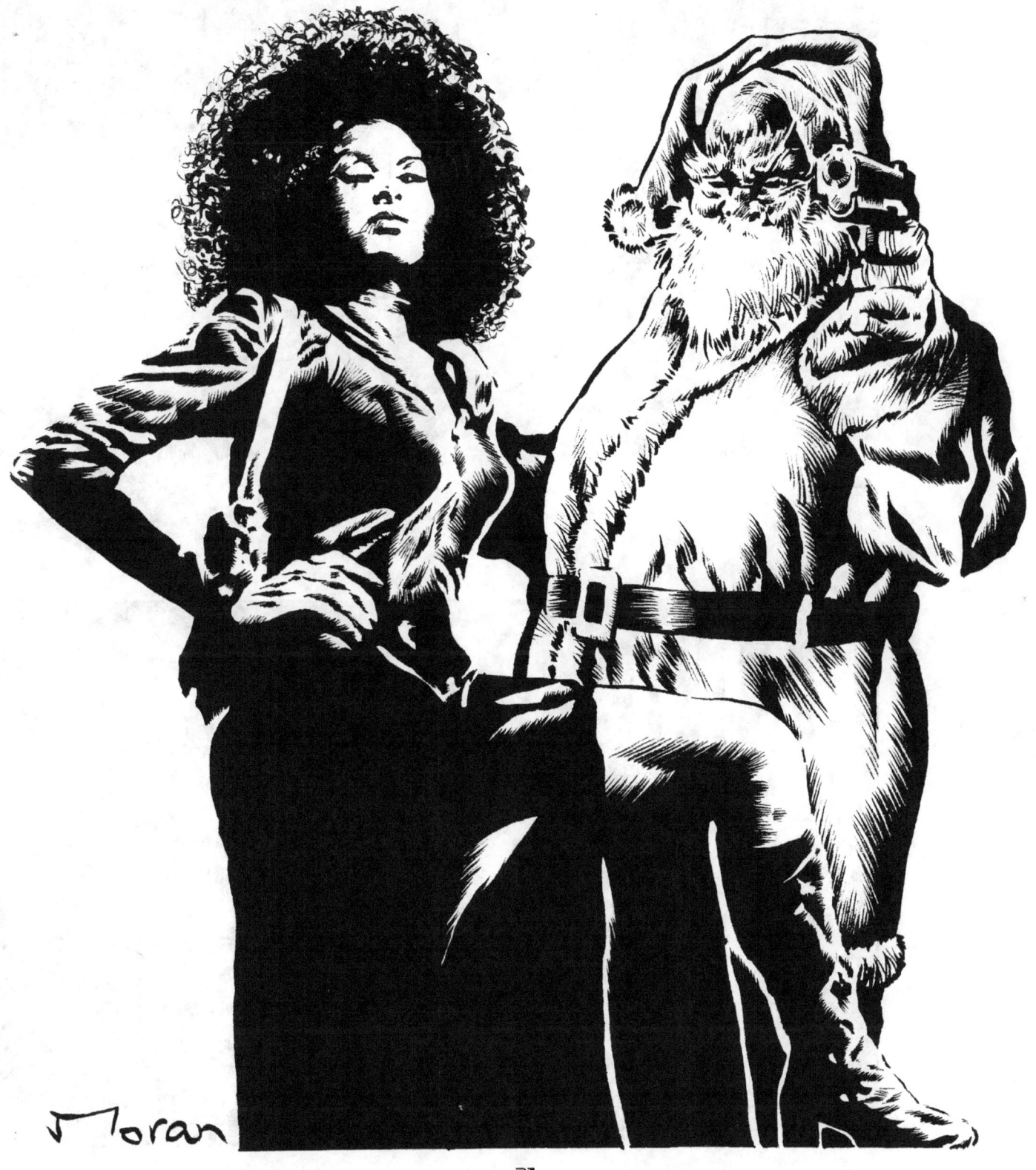

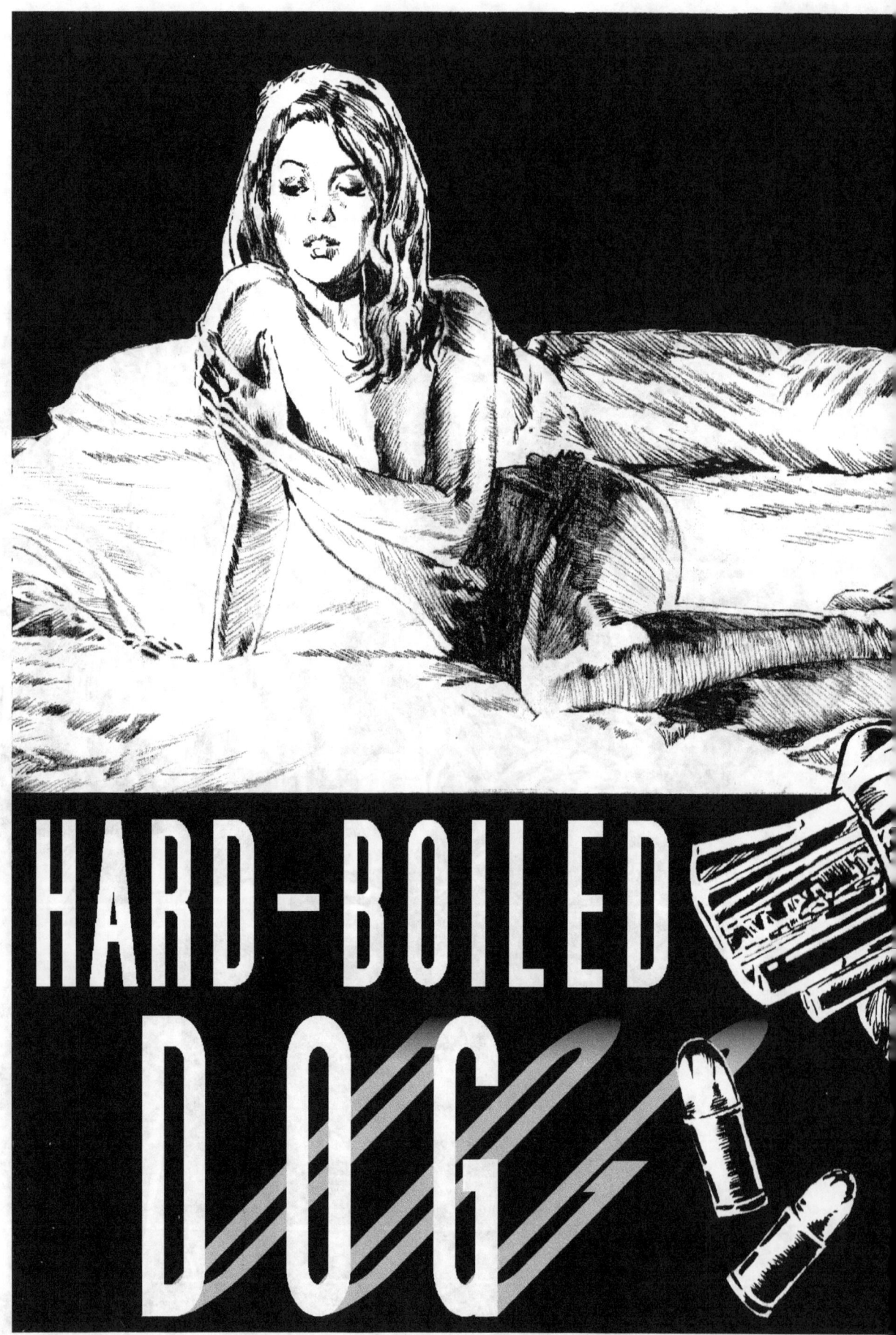

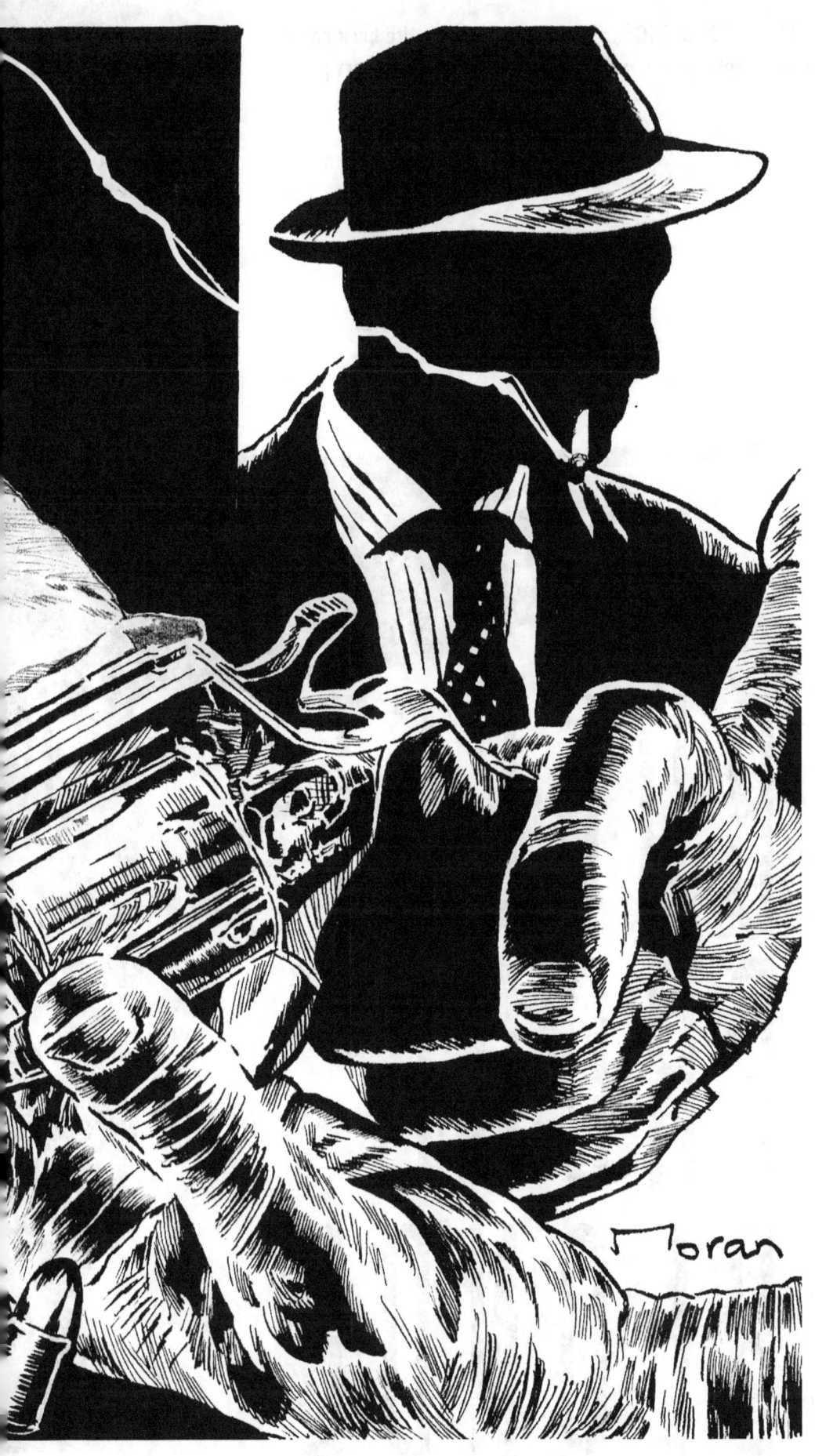

"My beautiful BULLET-PROOF BLONDE...I'm going to do an entire book about her one day; maybe a graphic novel, maybe a book of illustrated short prose stories."   —RM

BULLET-PROOF BLONDE

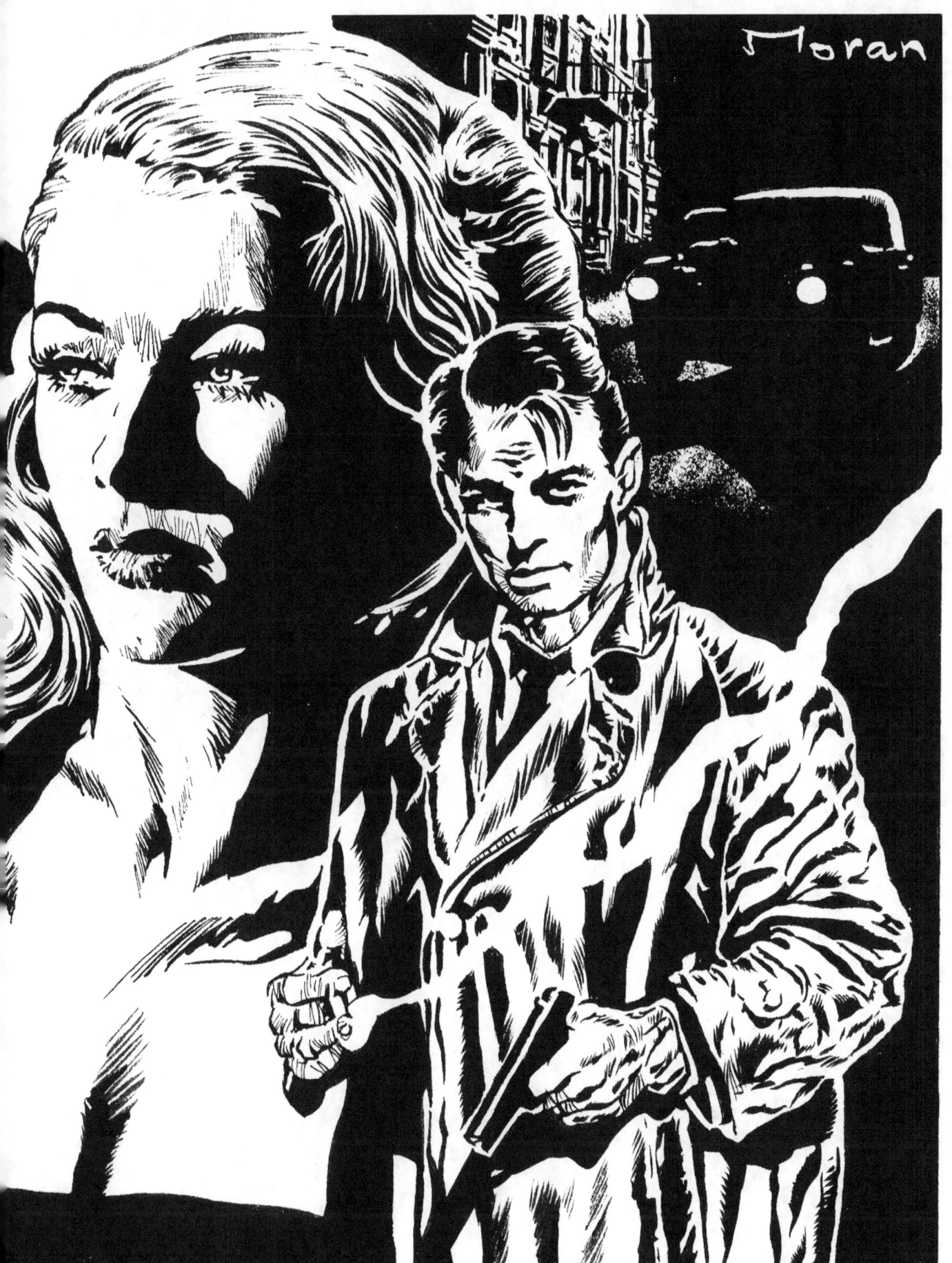

35

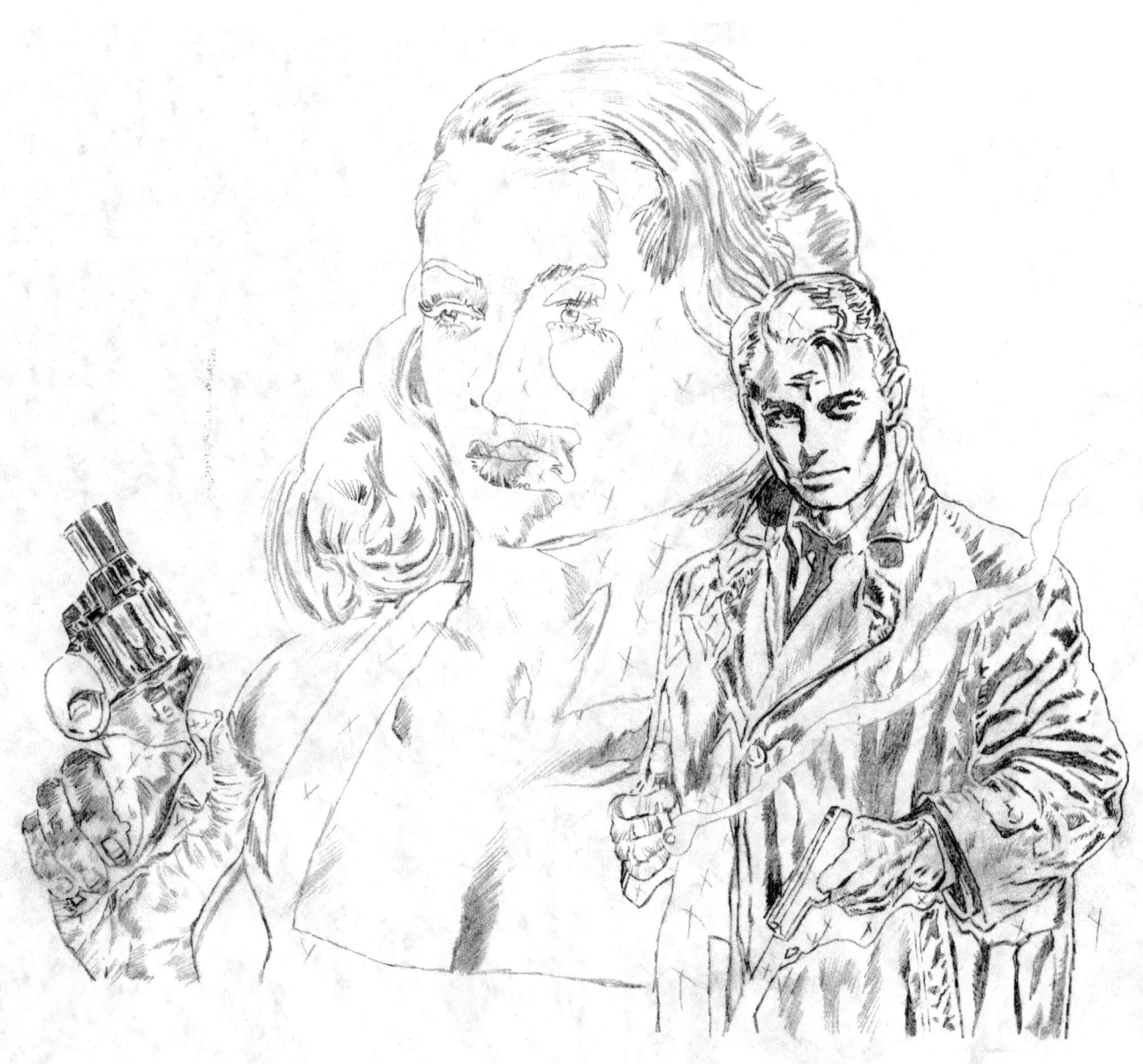

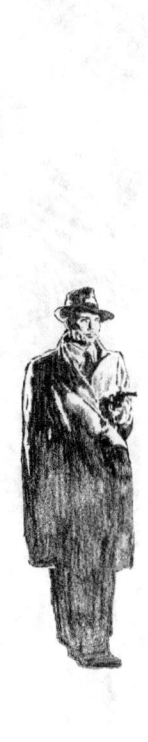
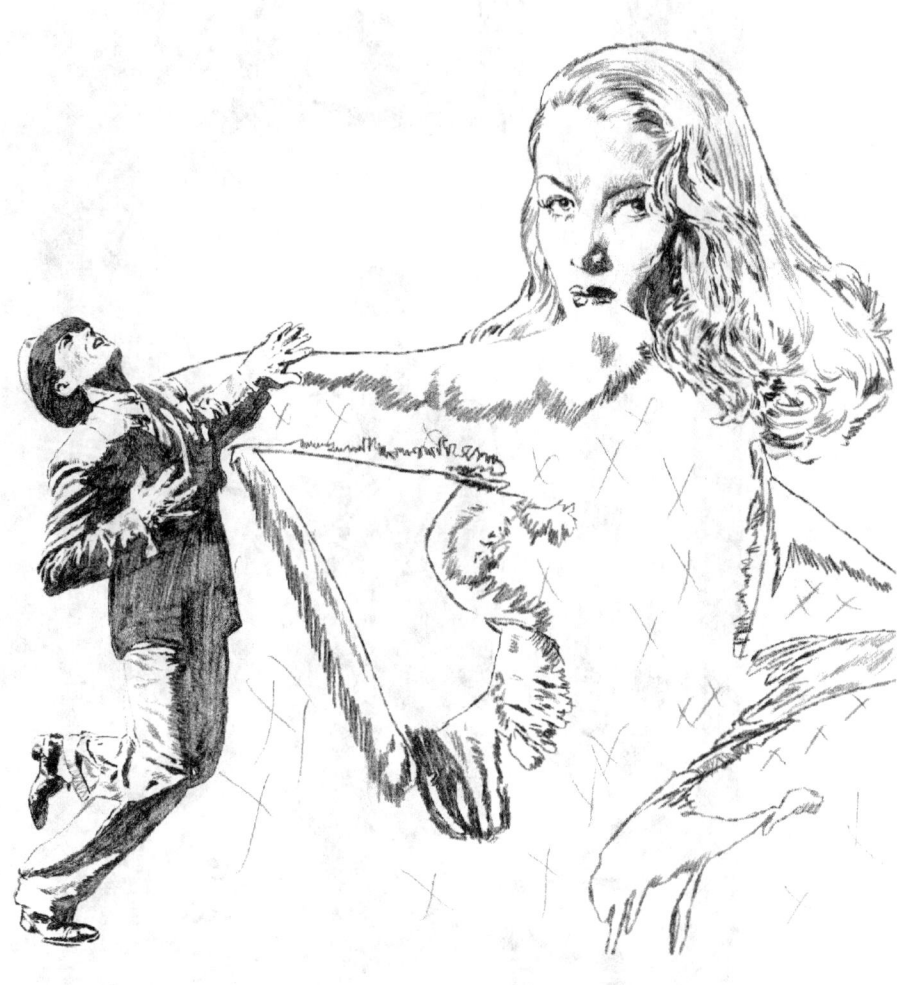

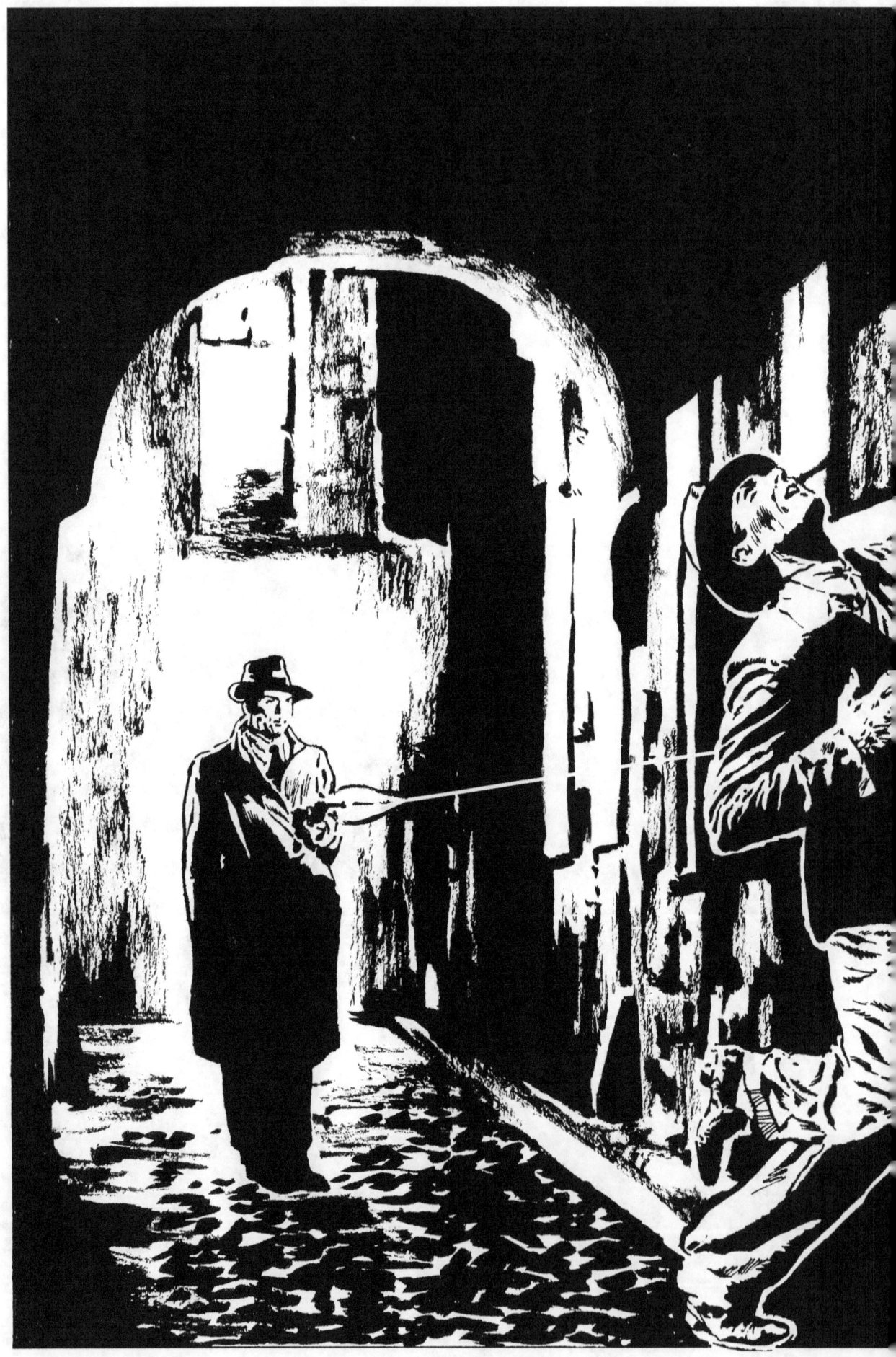

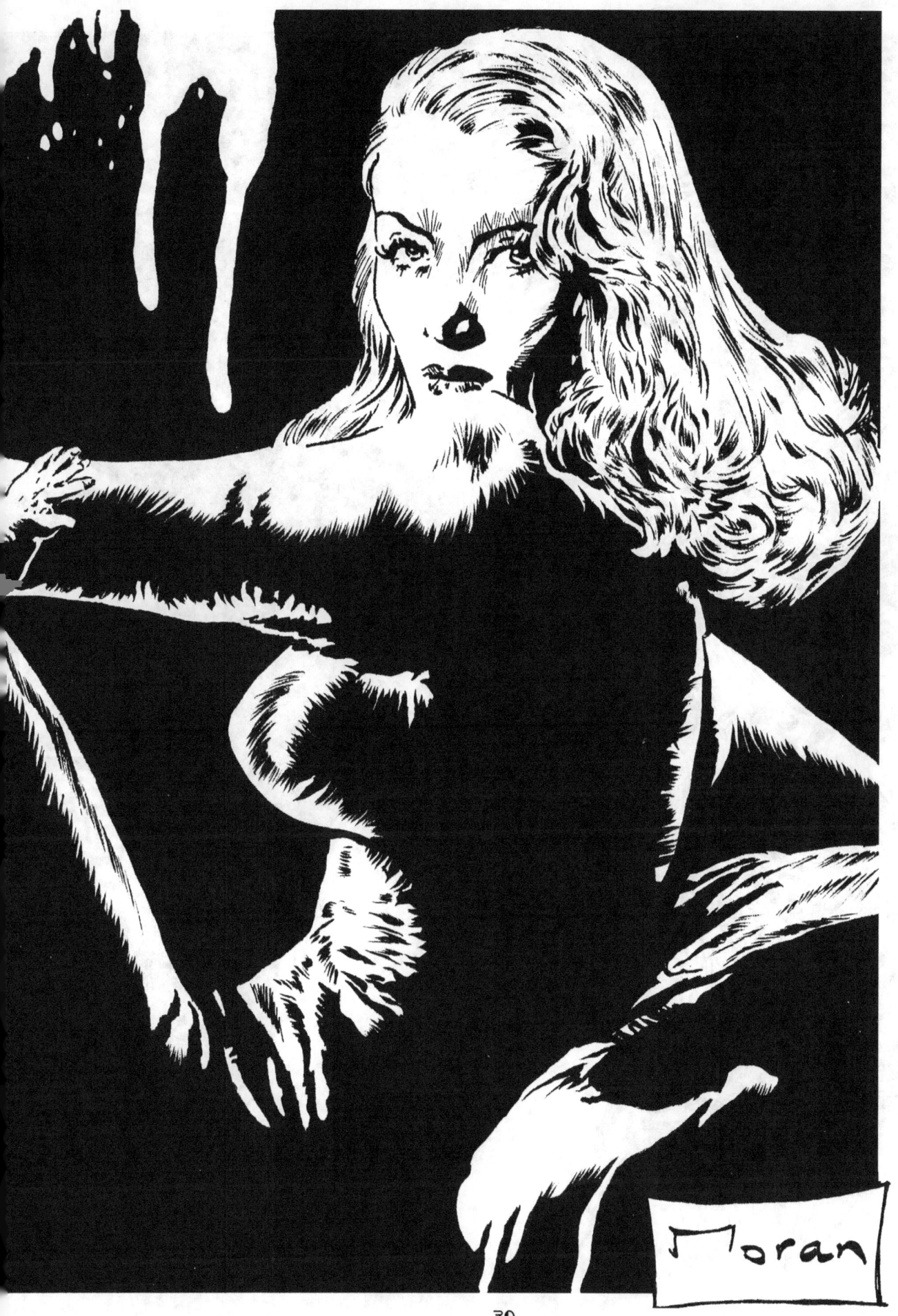

Moran

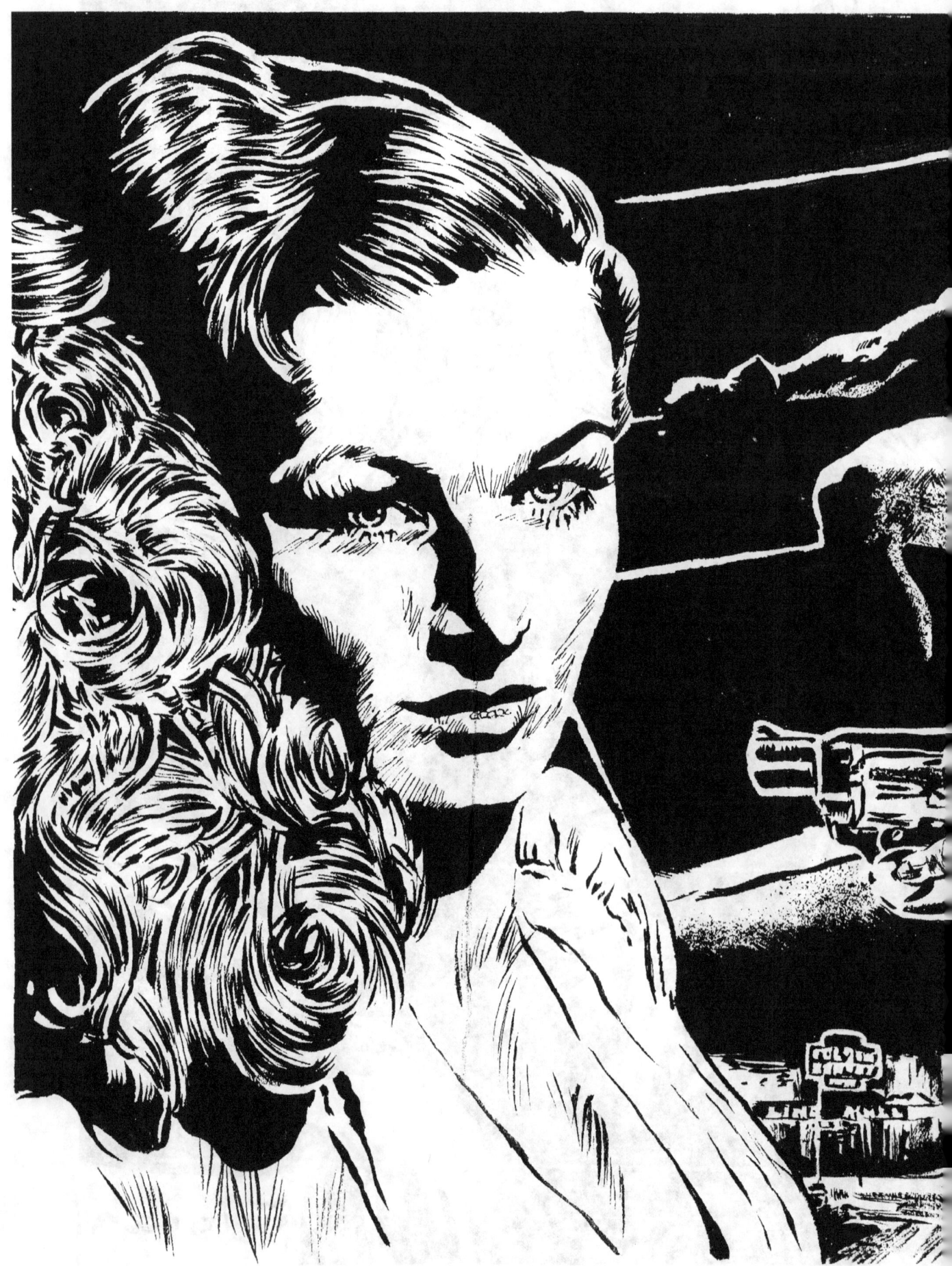

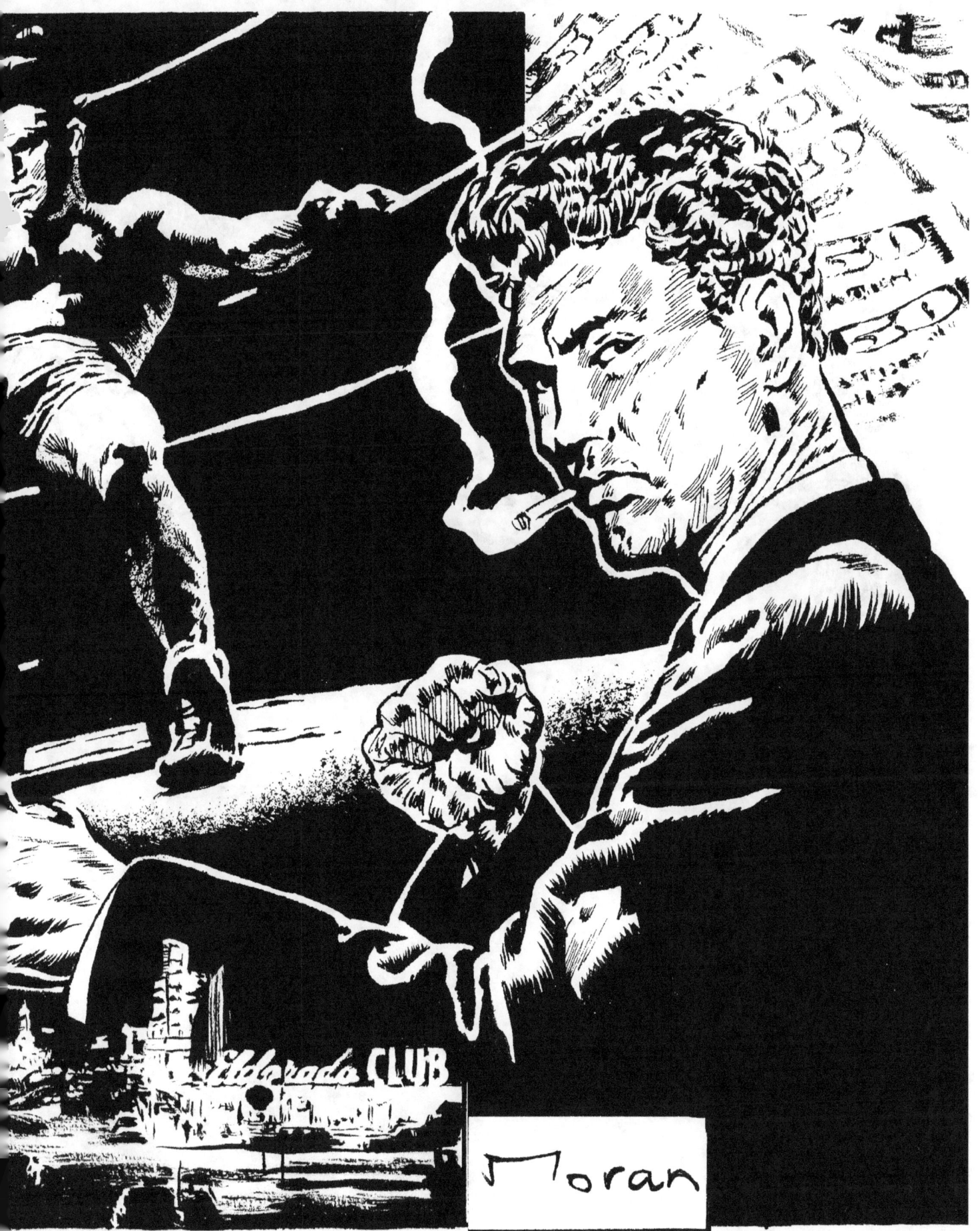

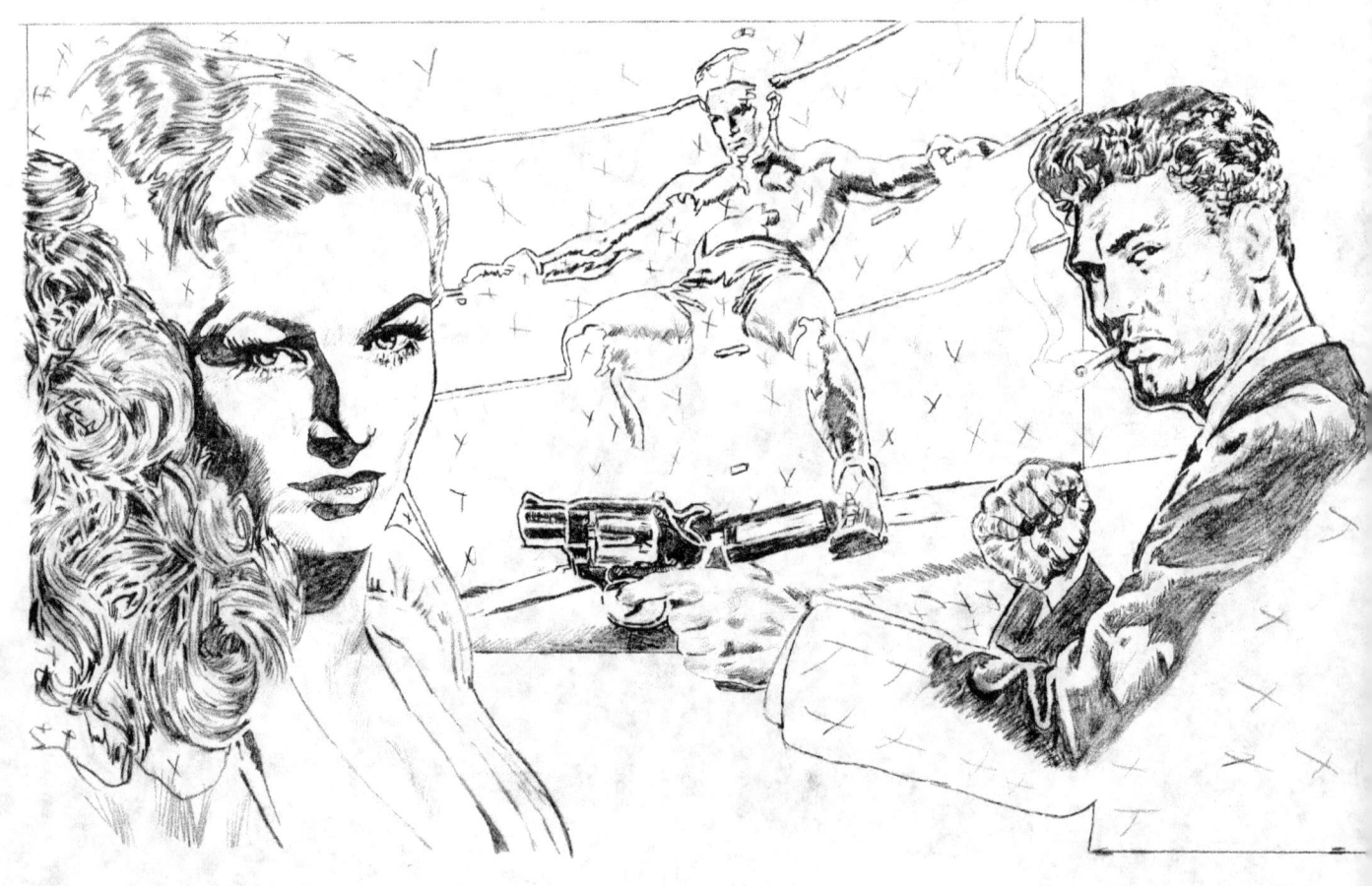

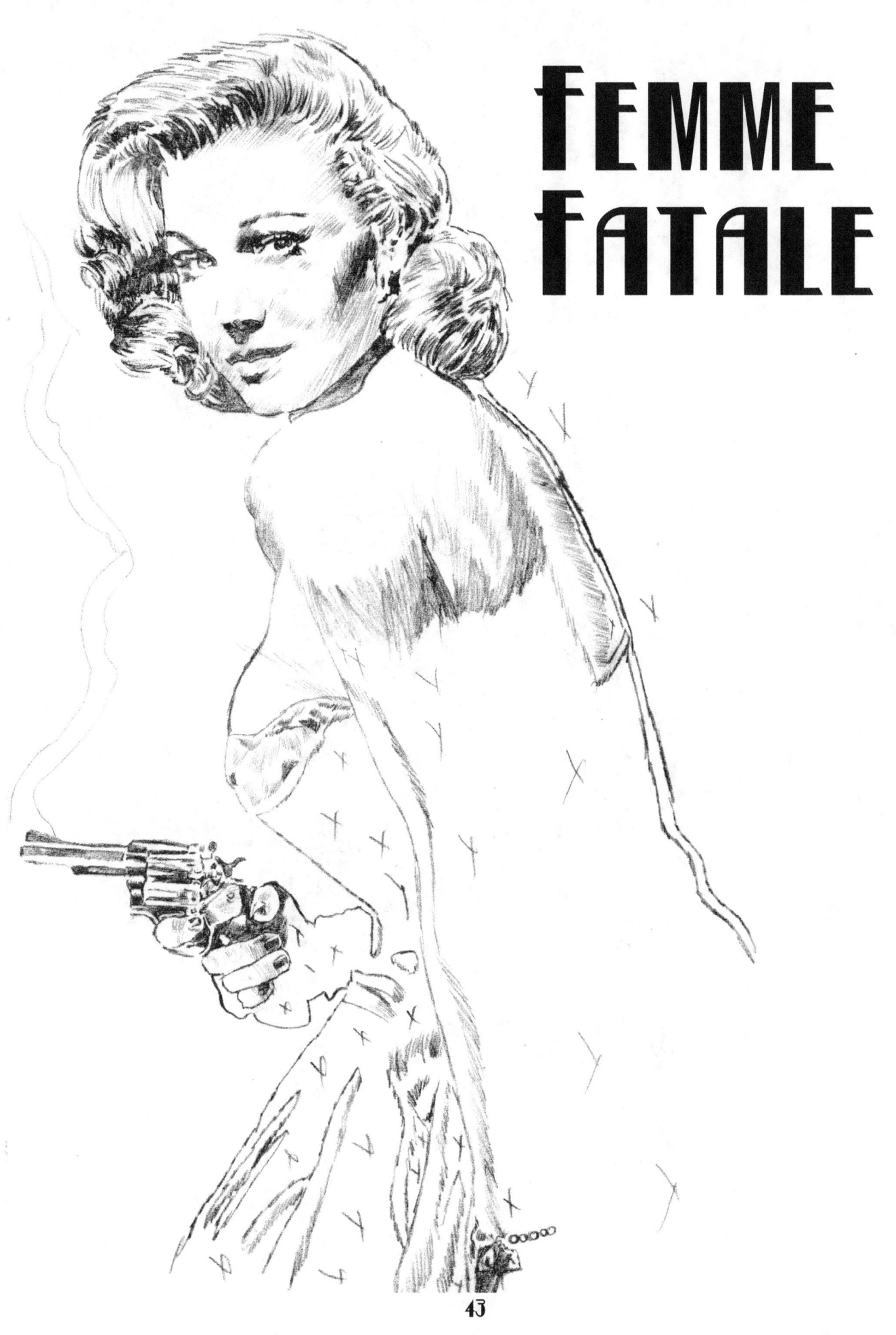

FEMME FATALE

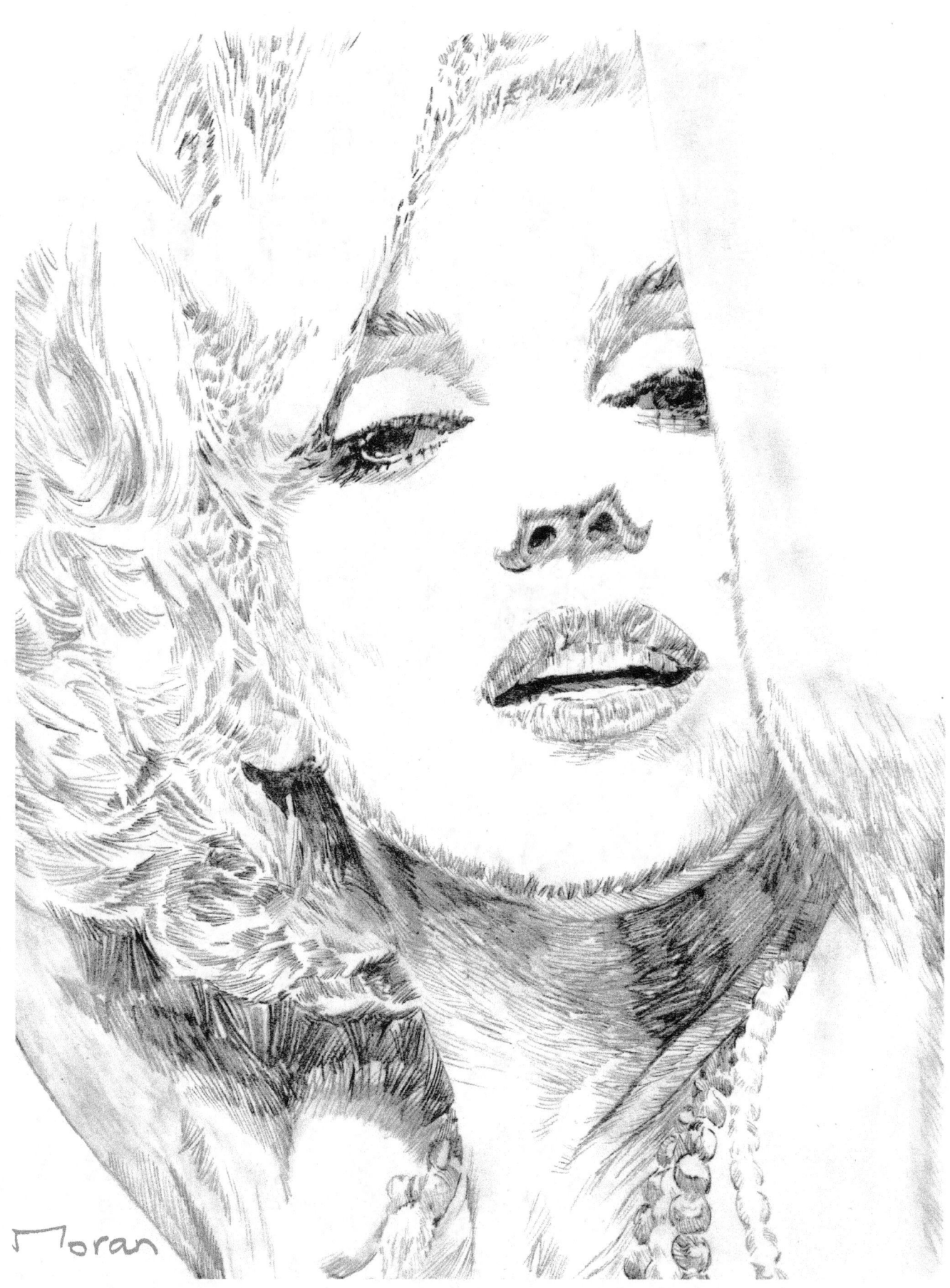

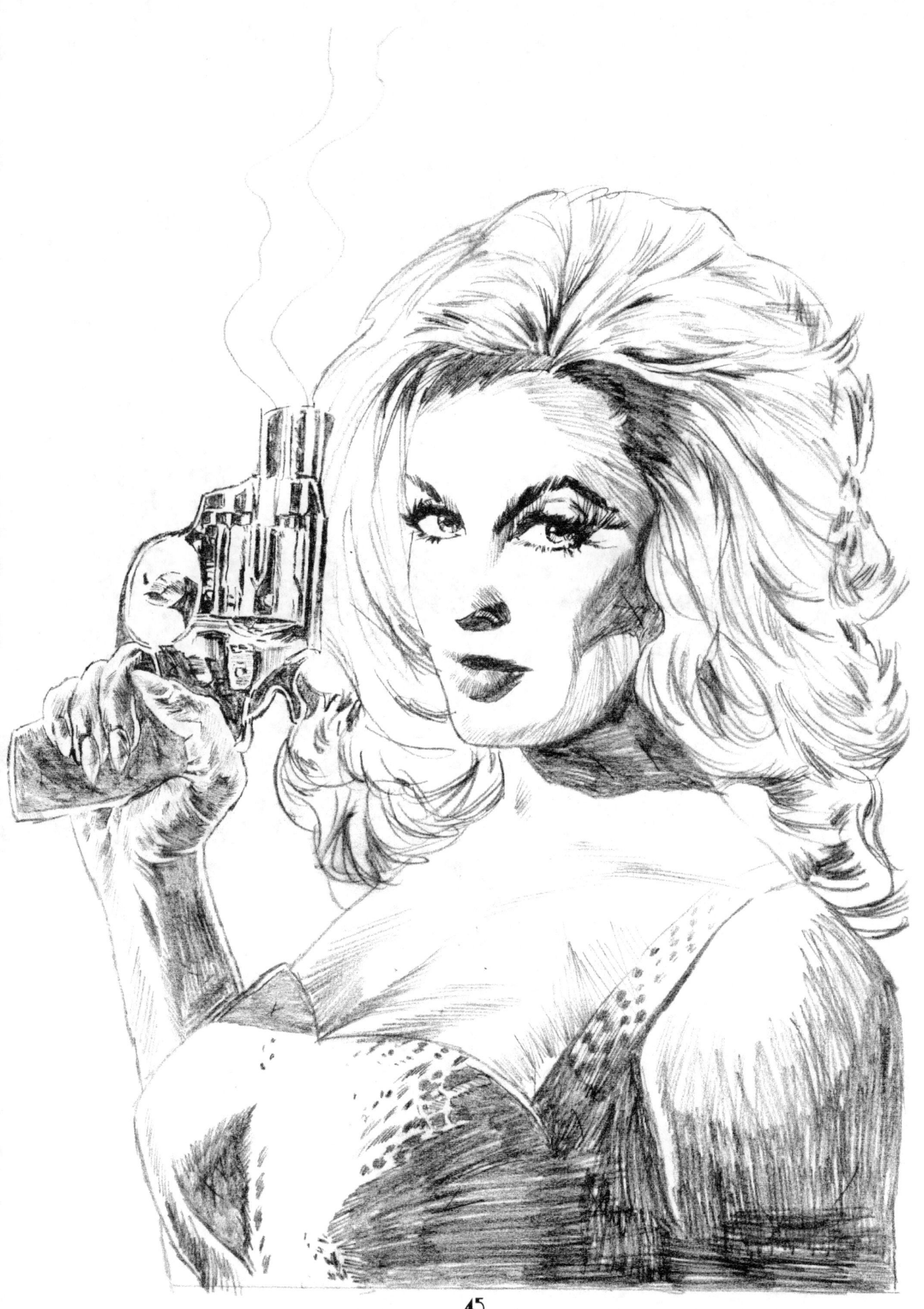

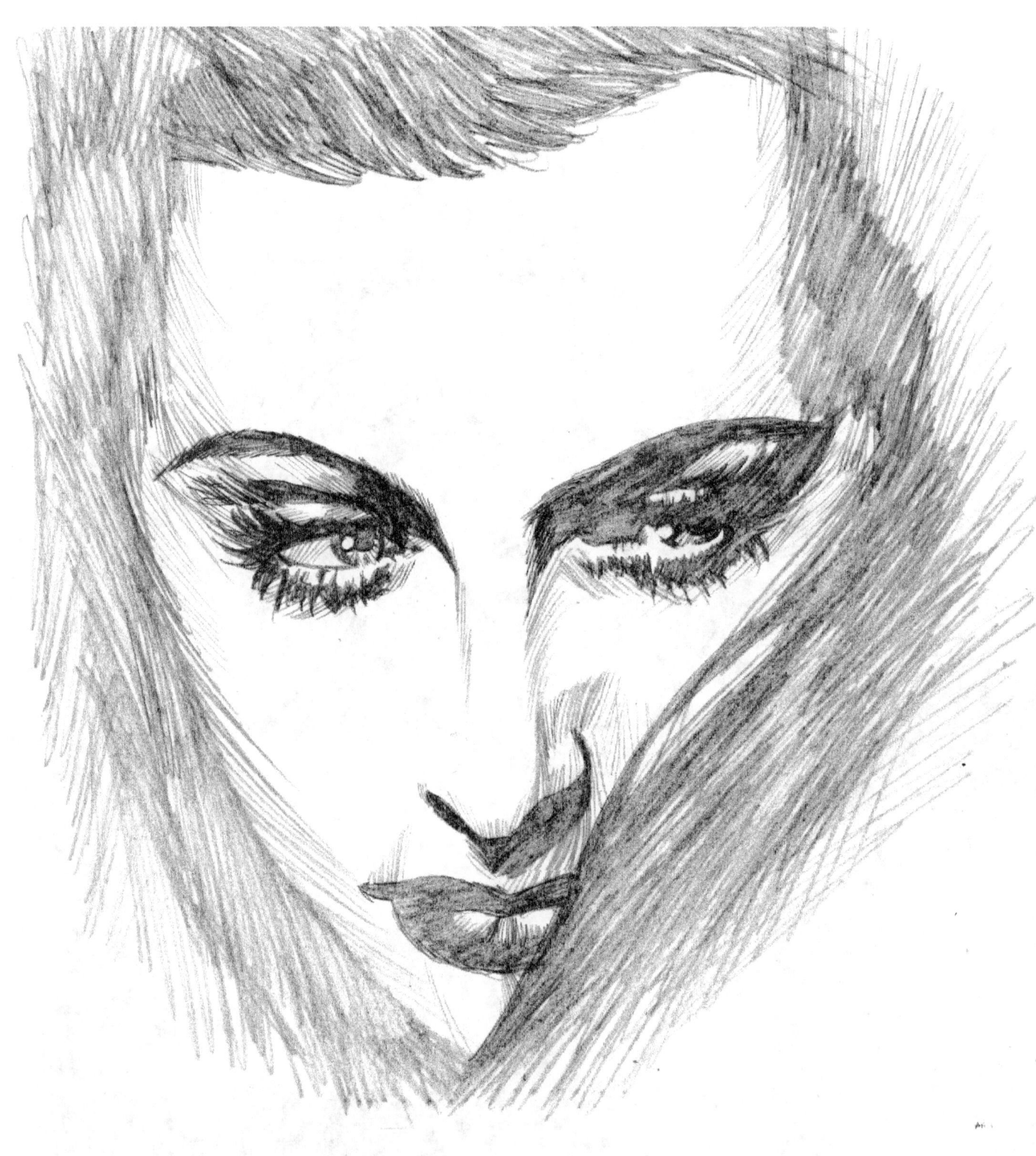

46

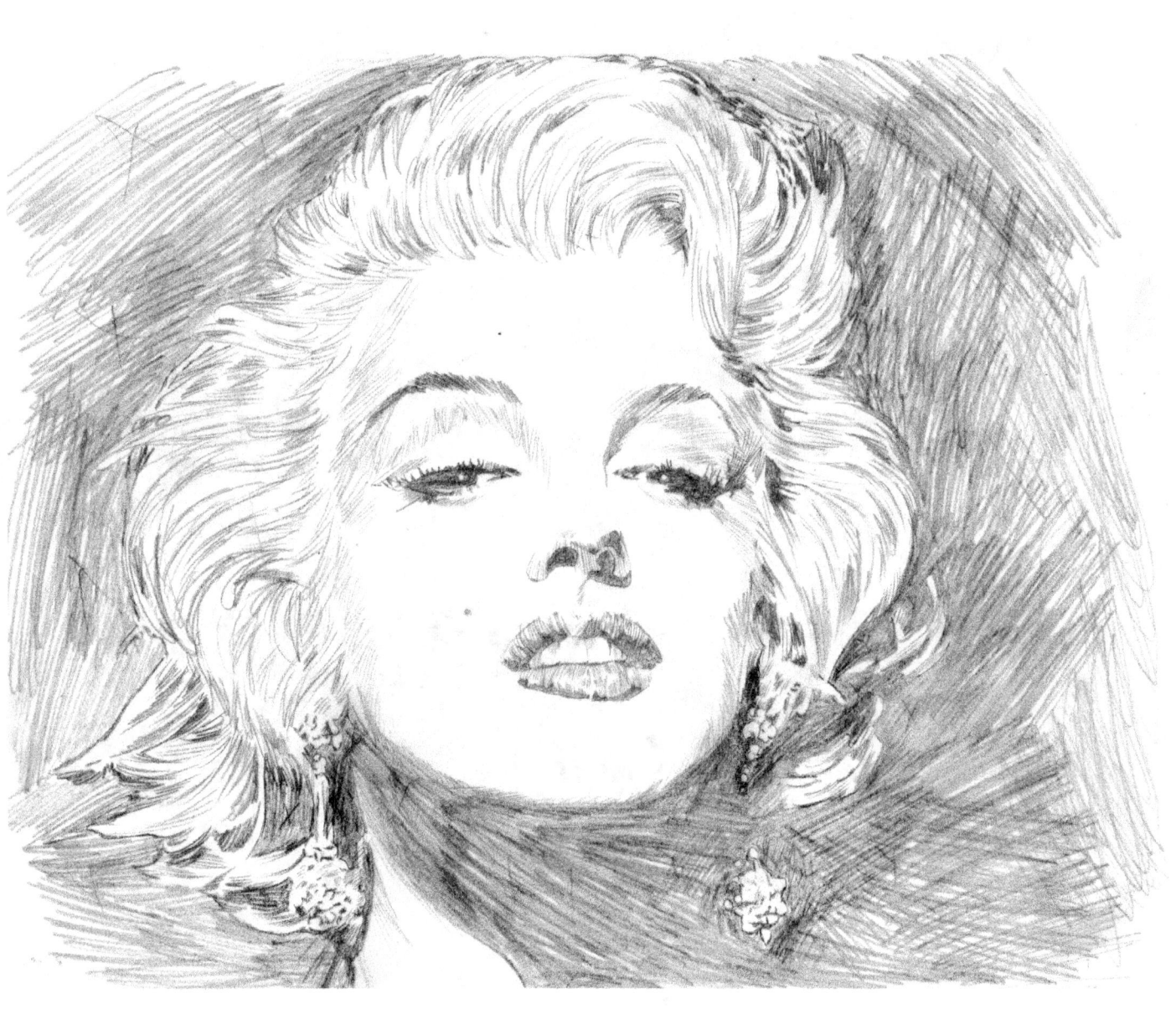

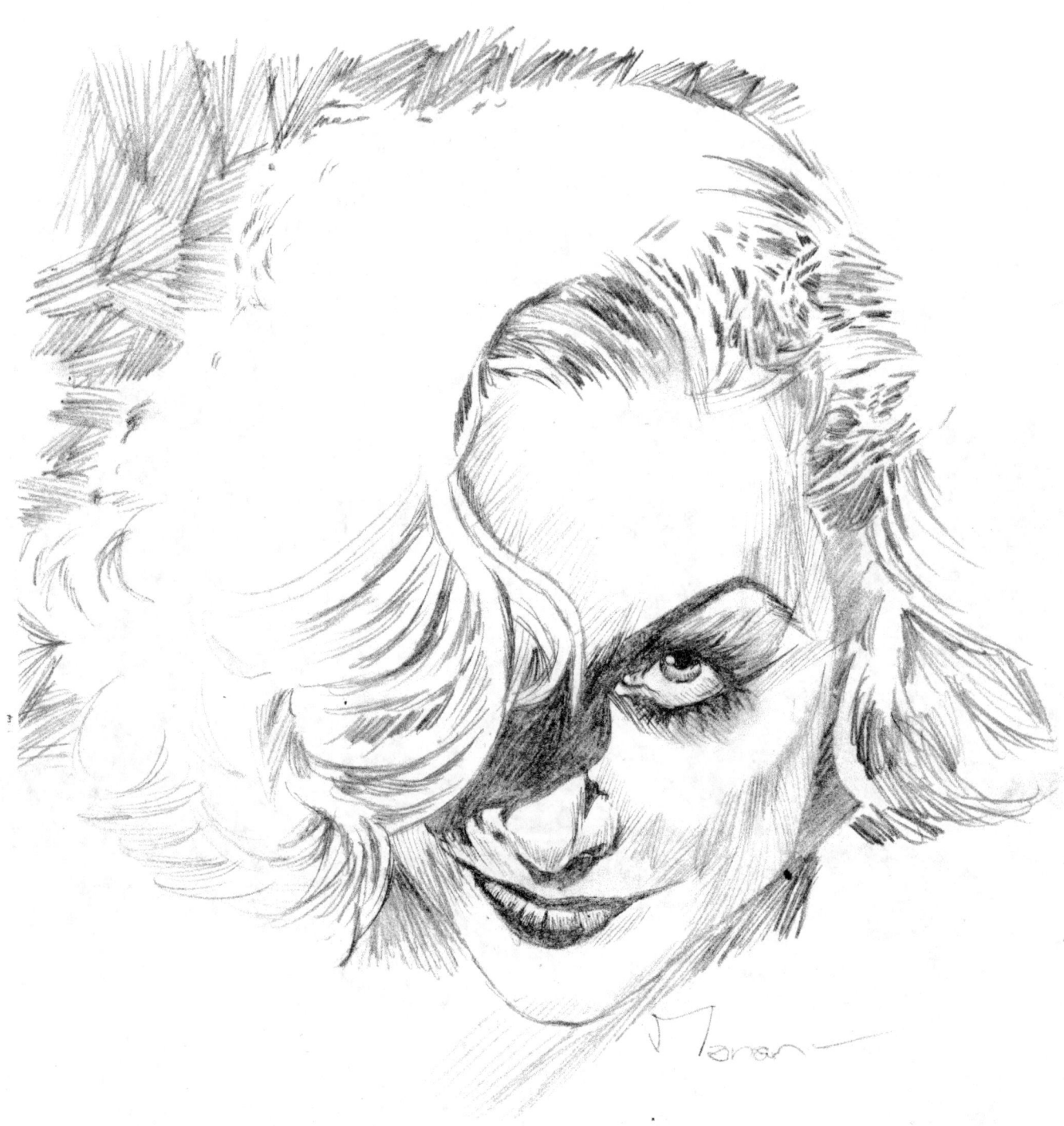

48

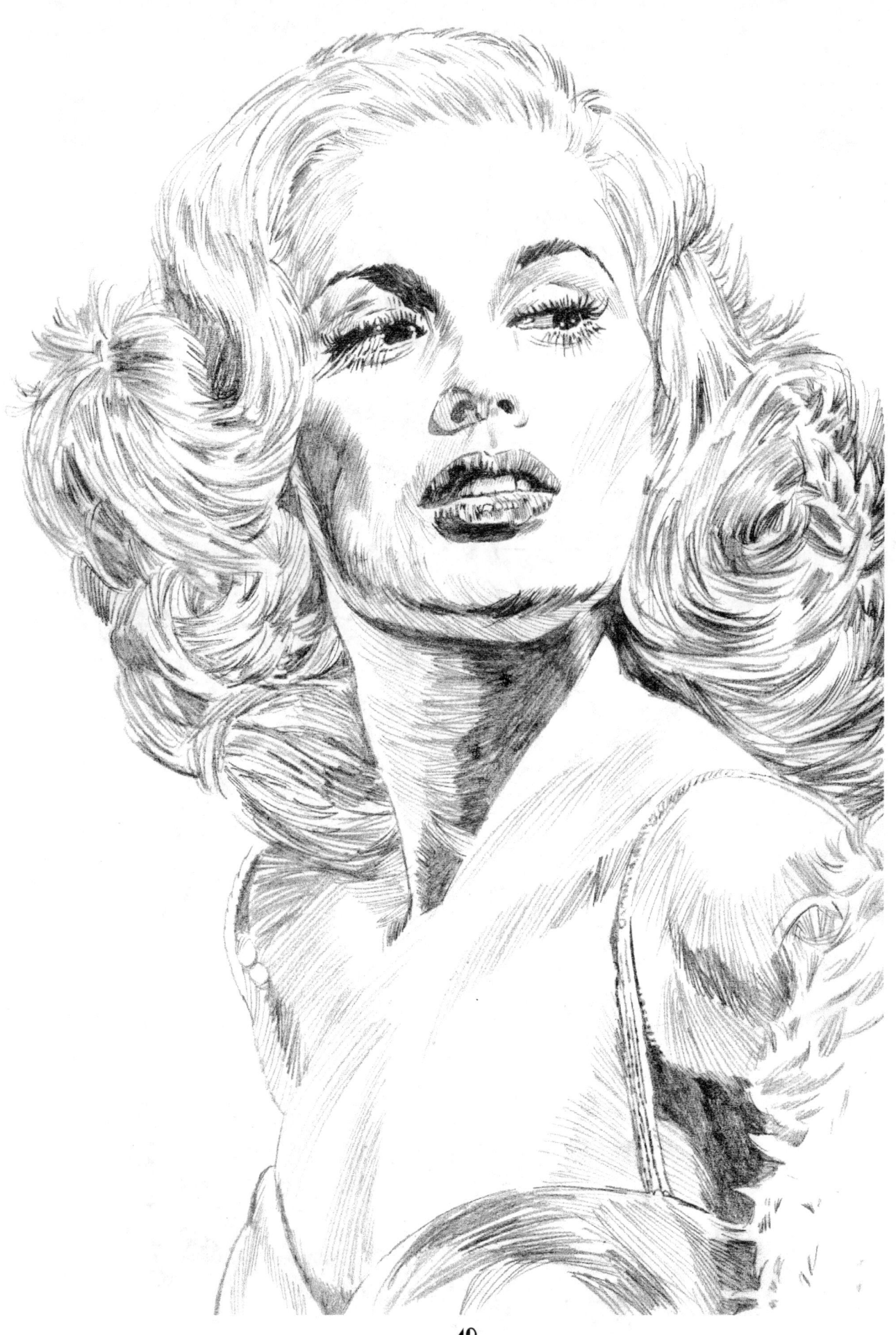

49

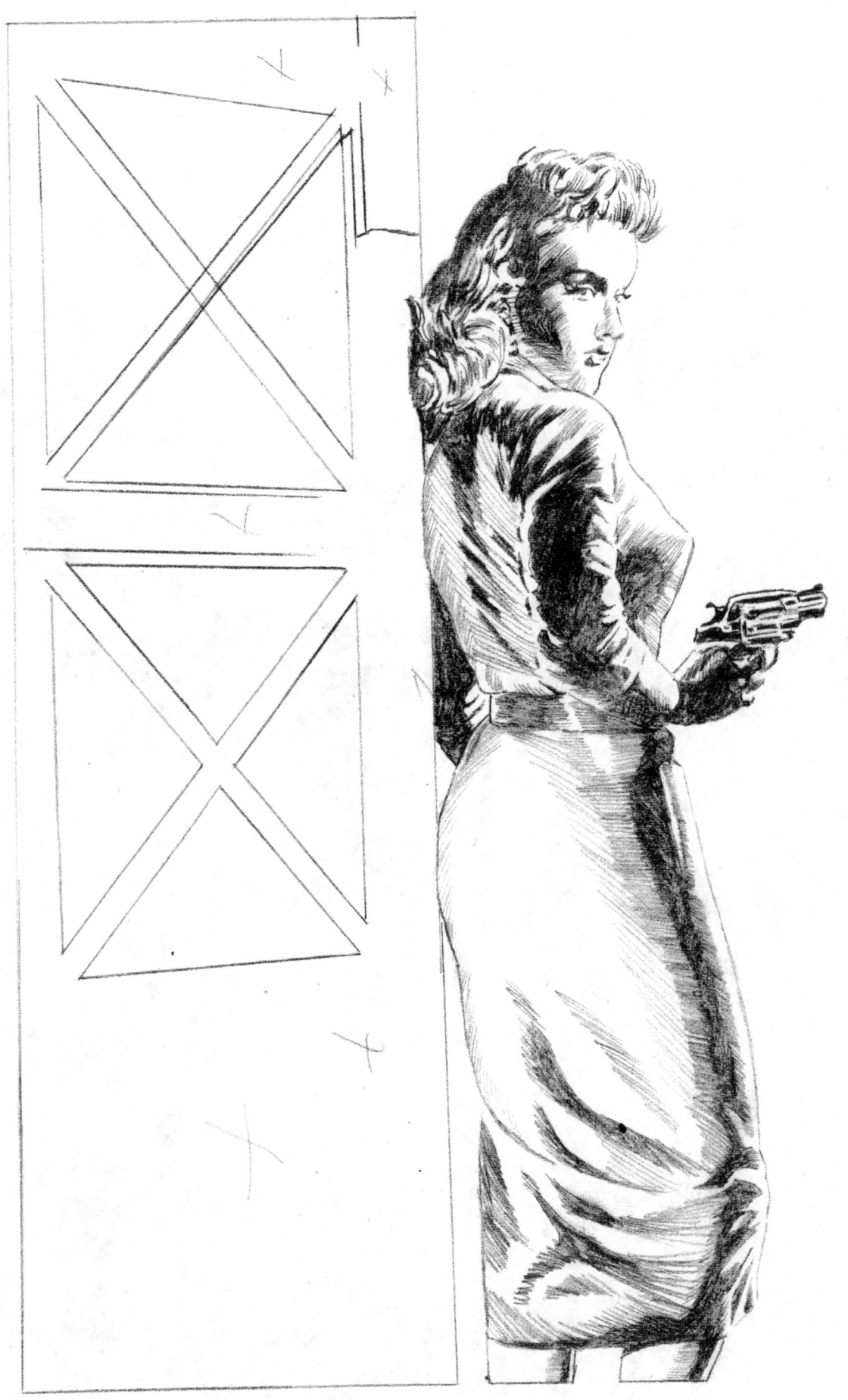

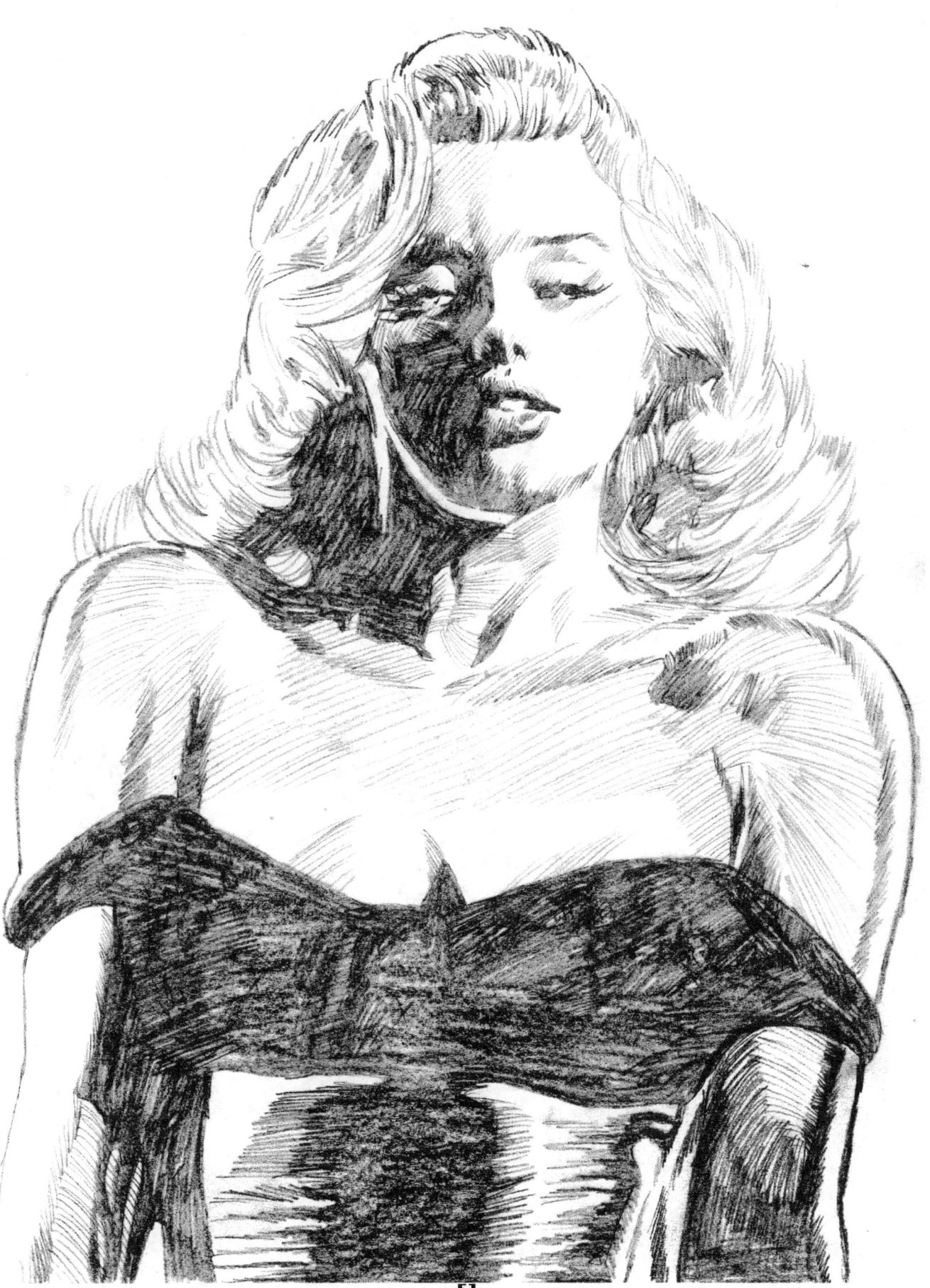

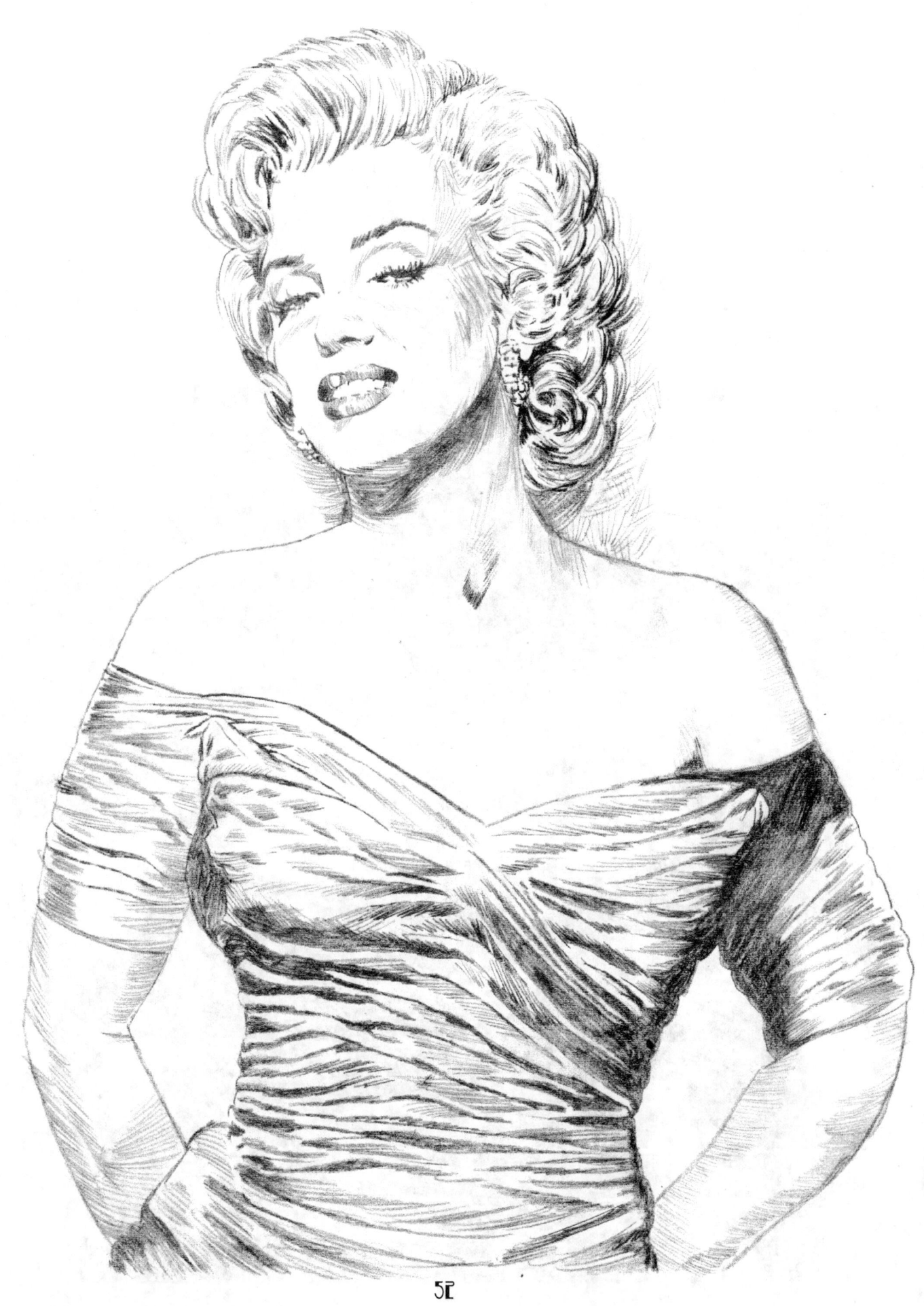

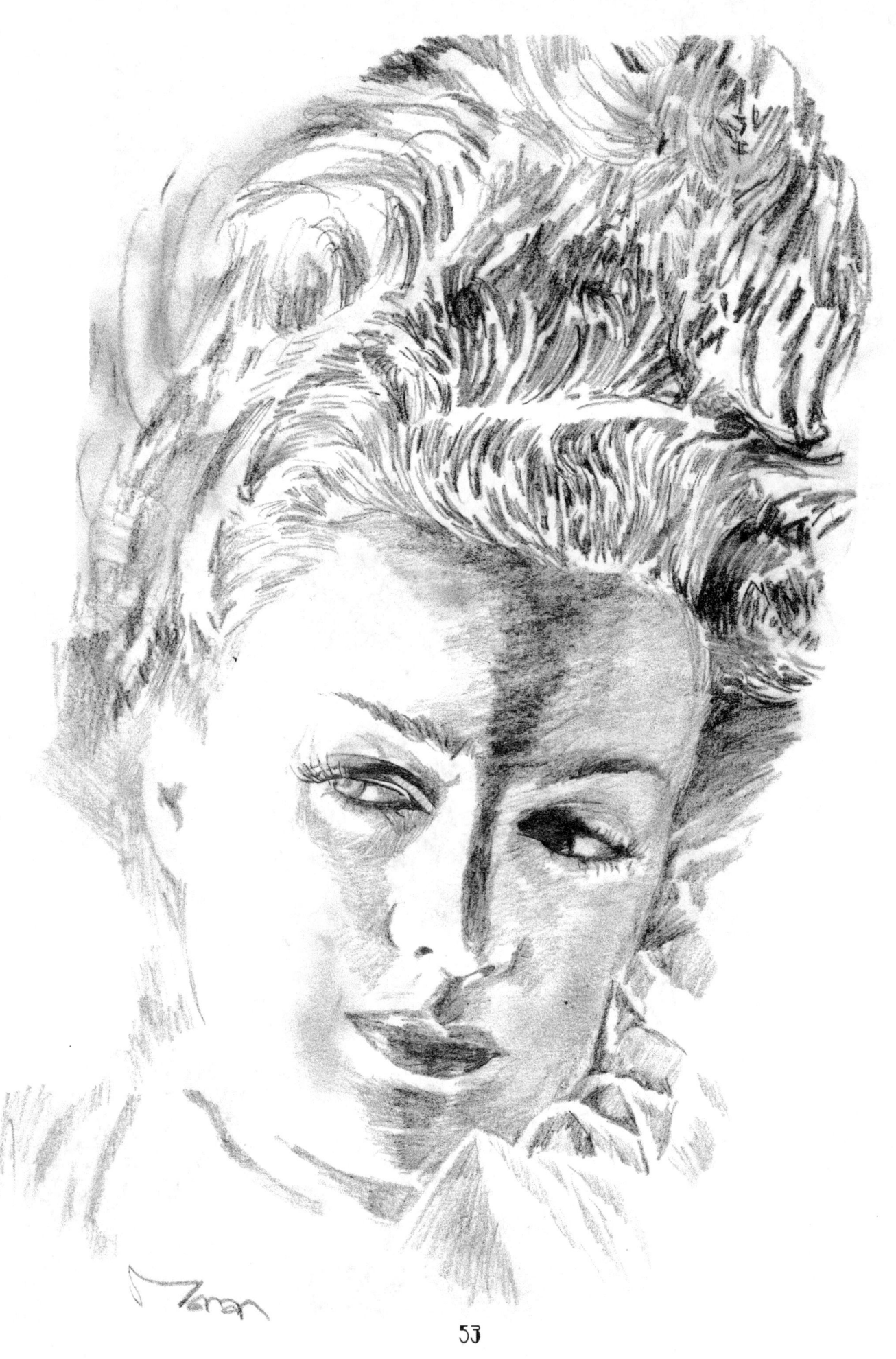

53

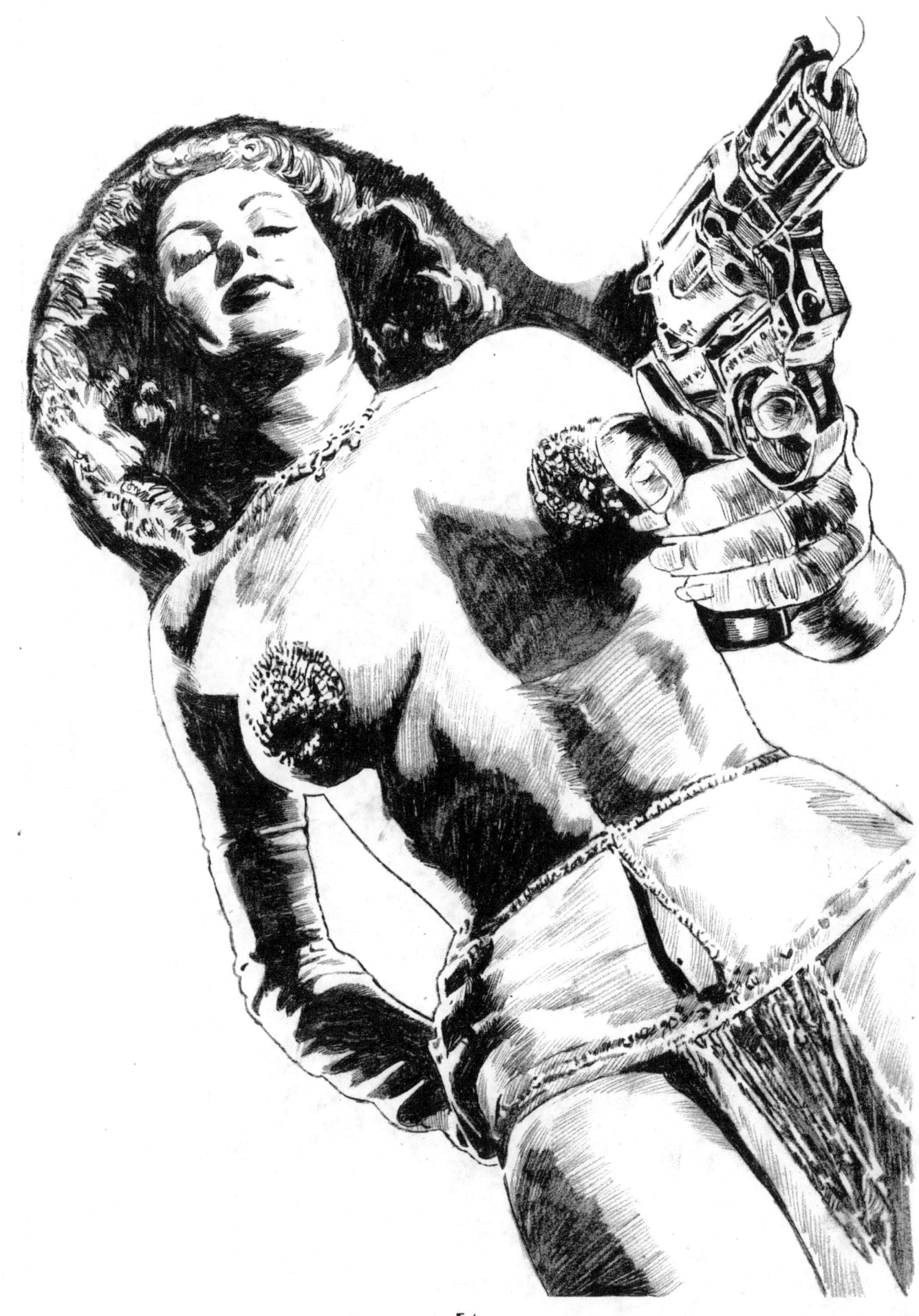

54

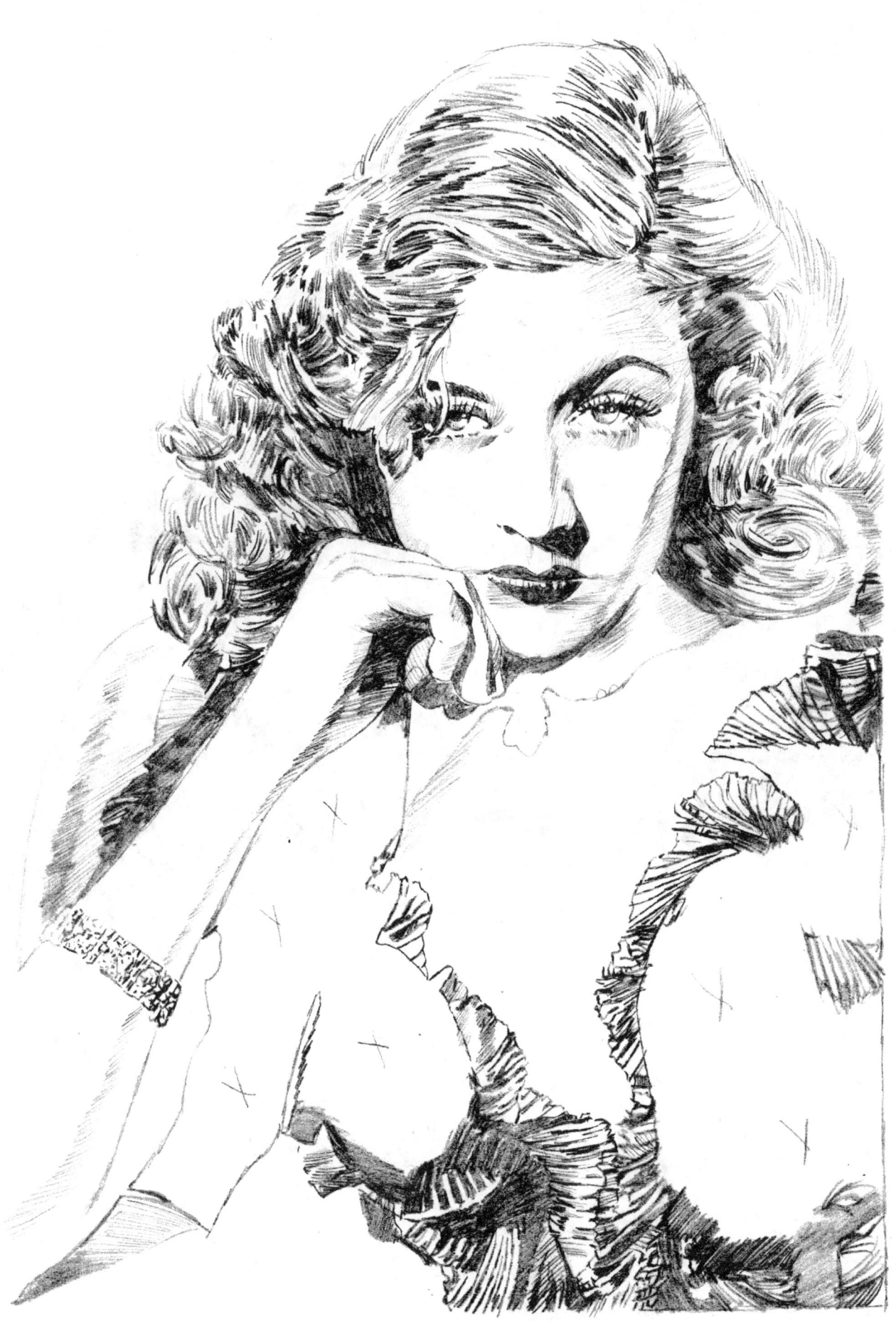

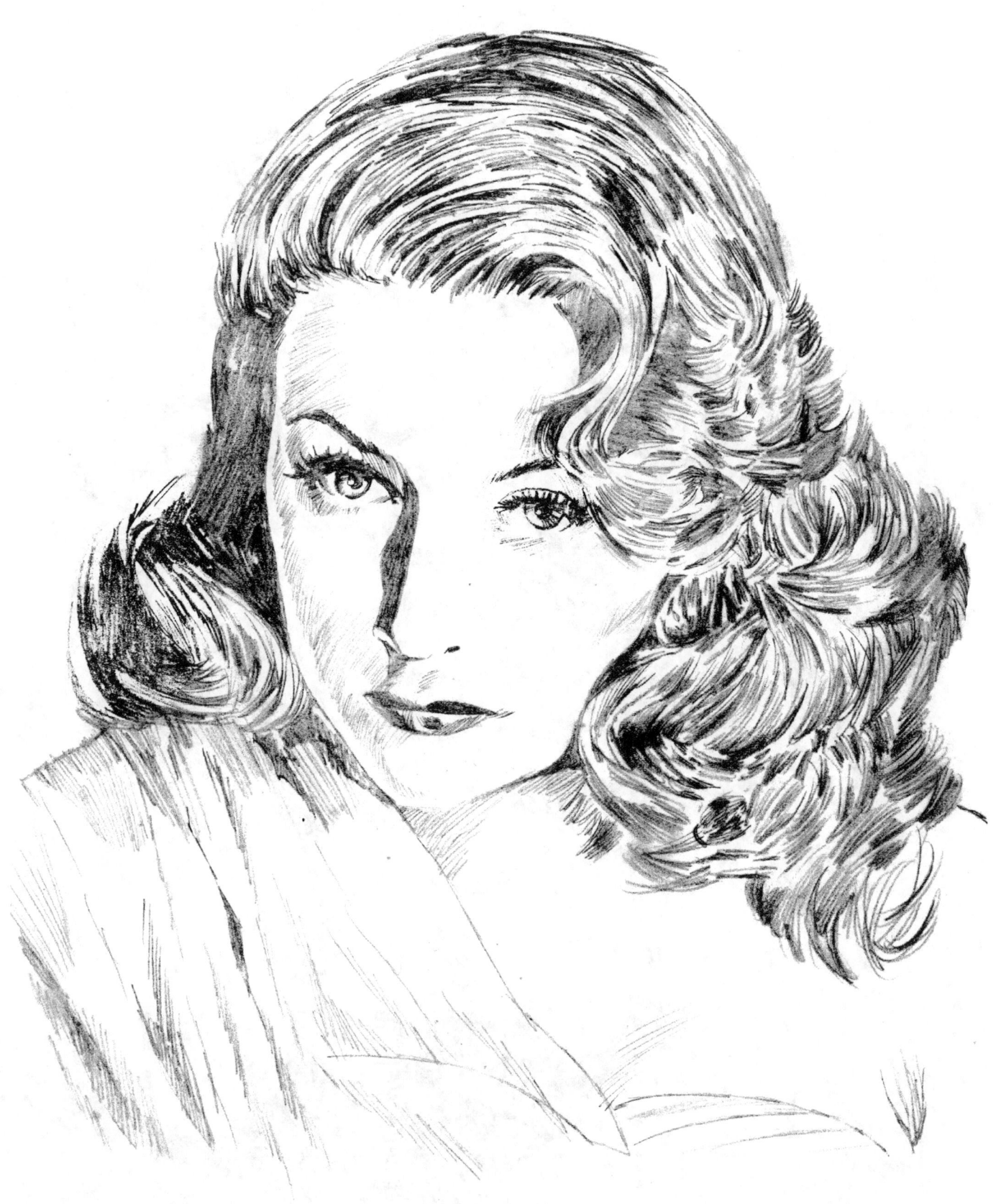

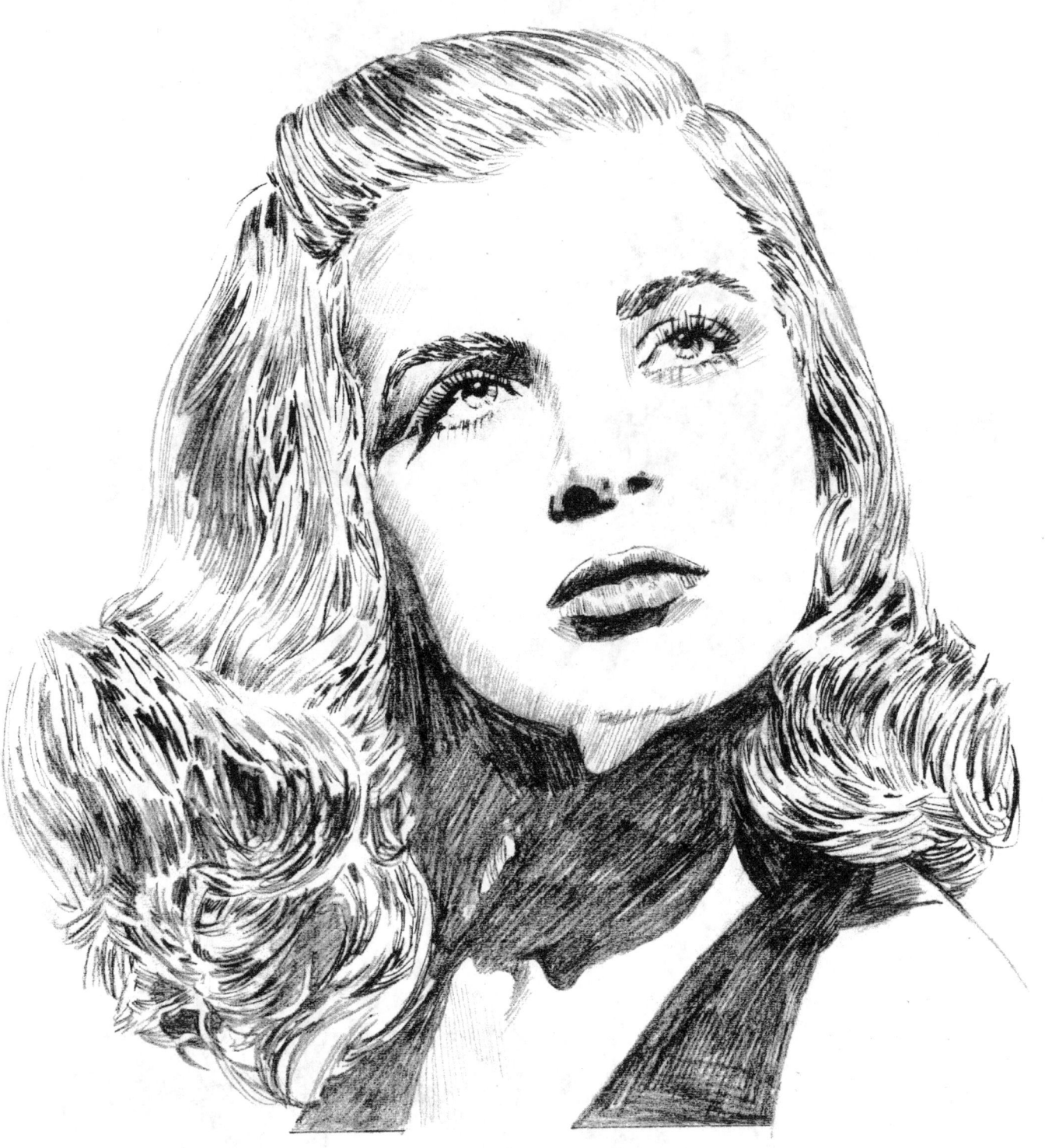

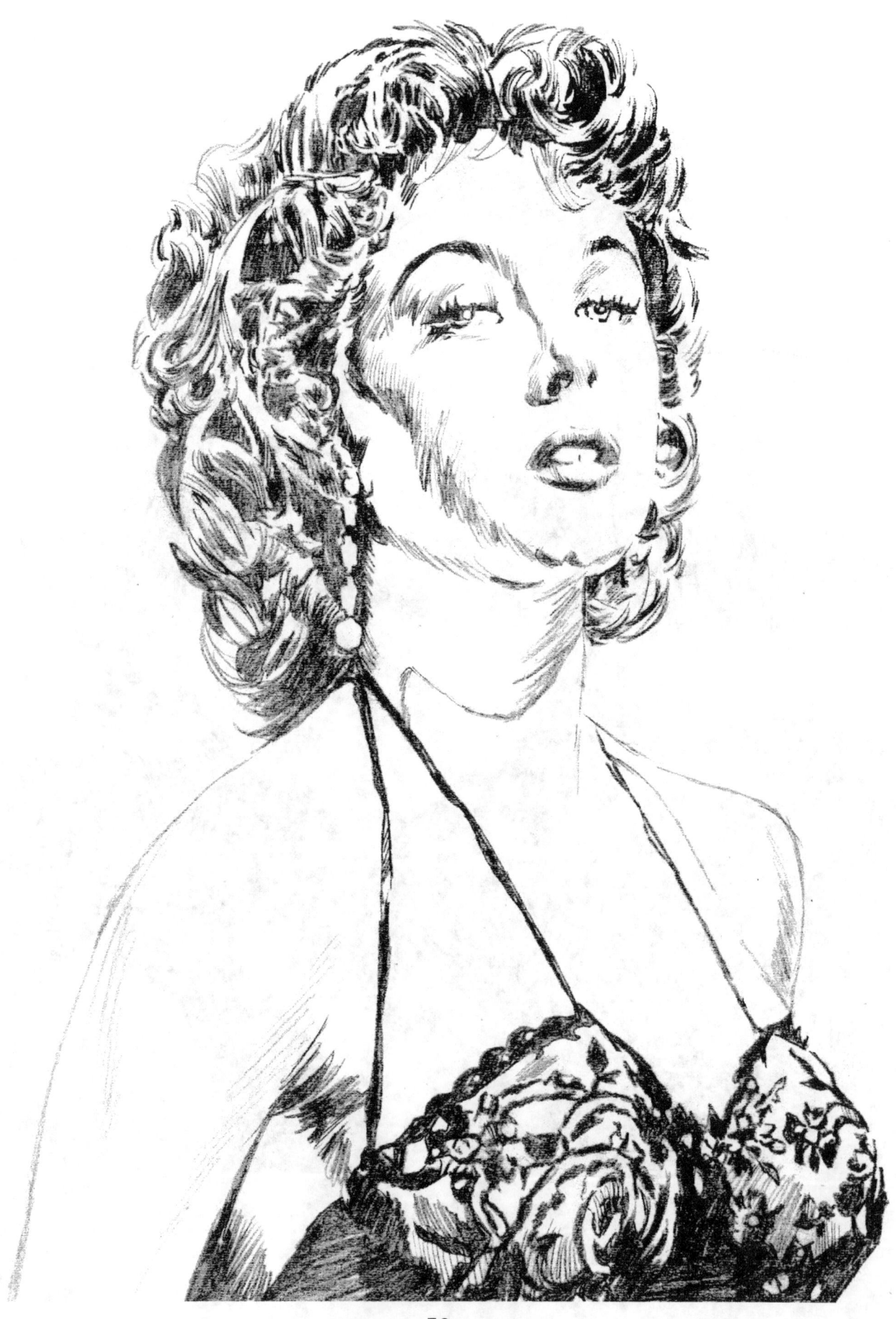

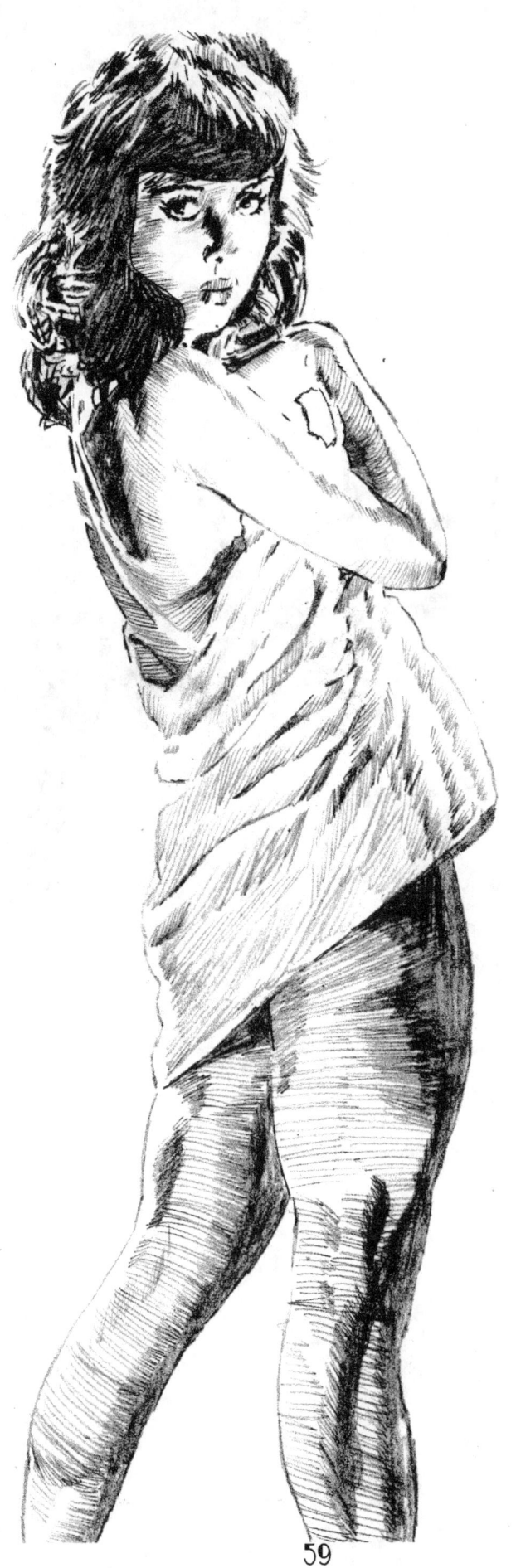

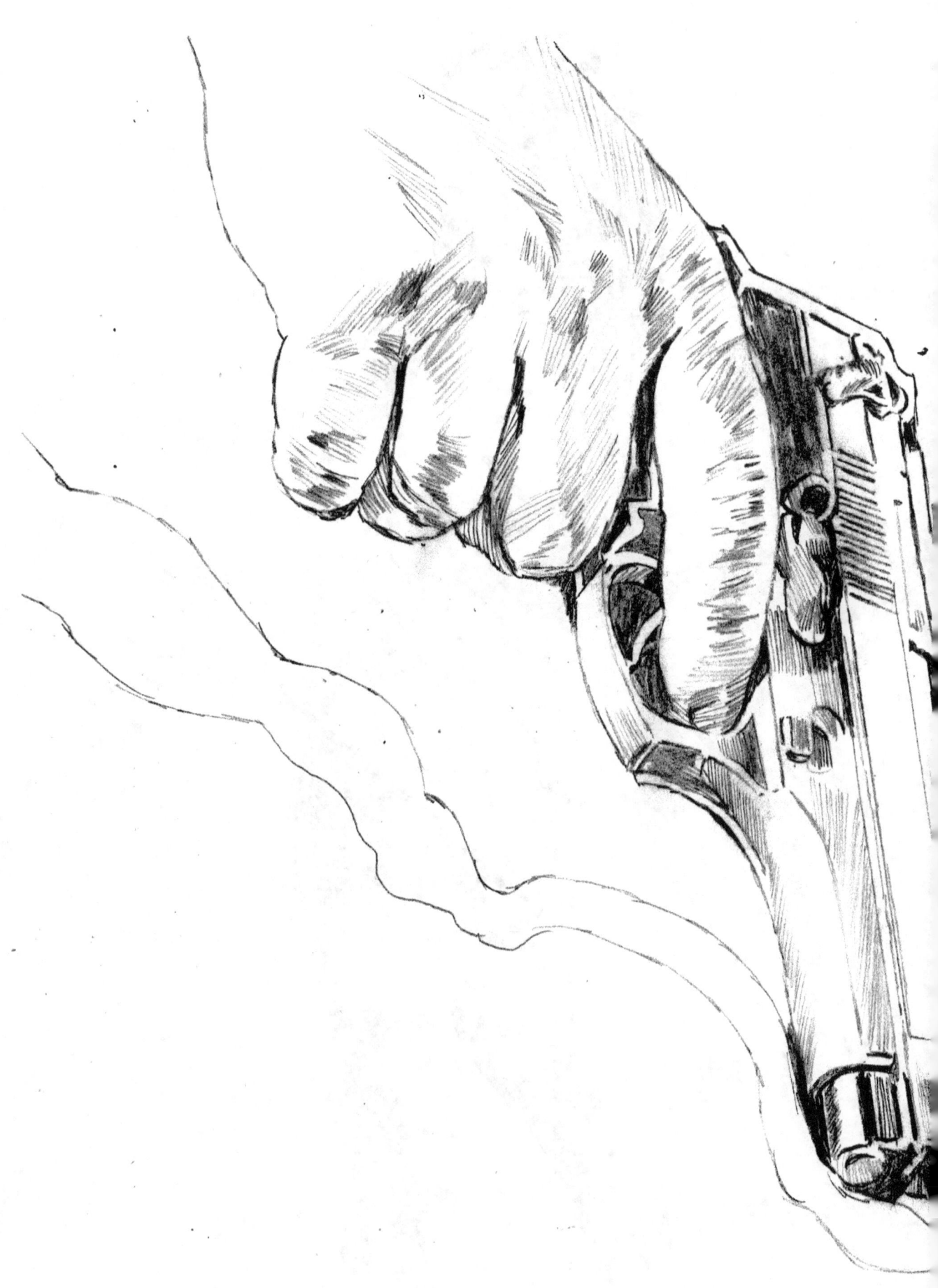

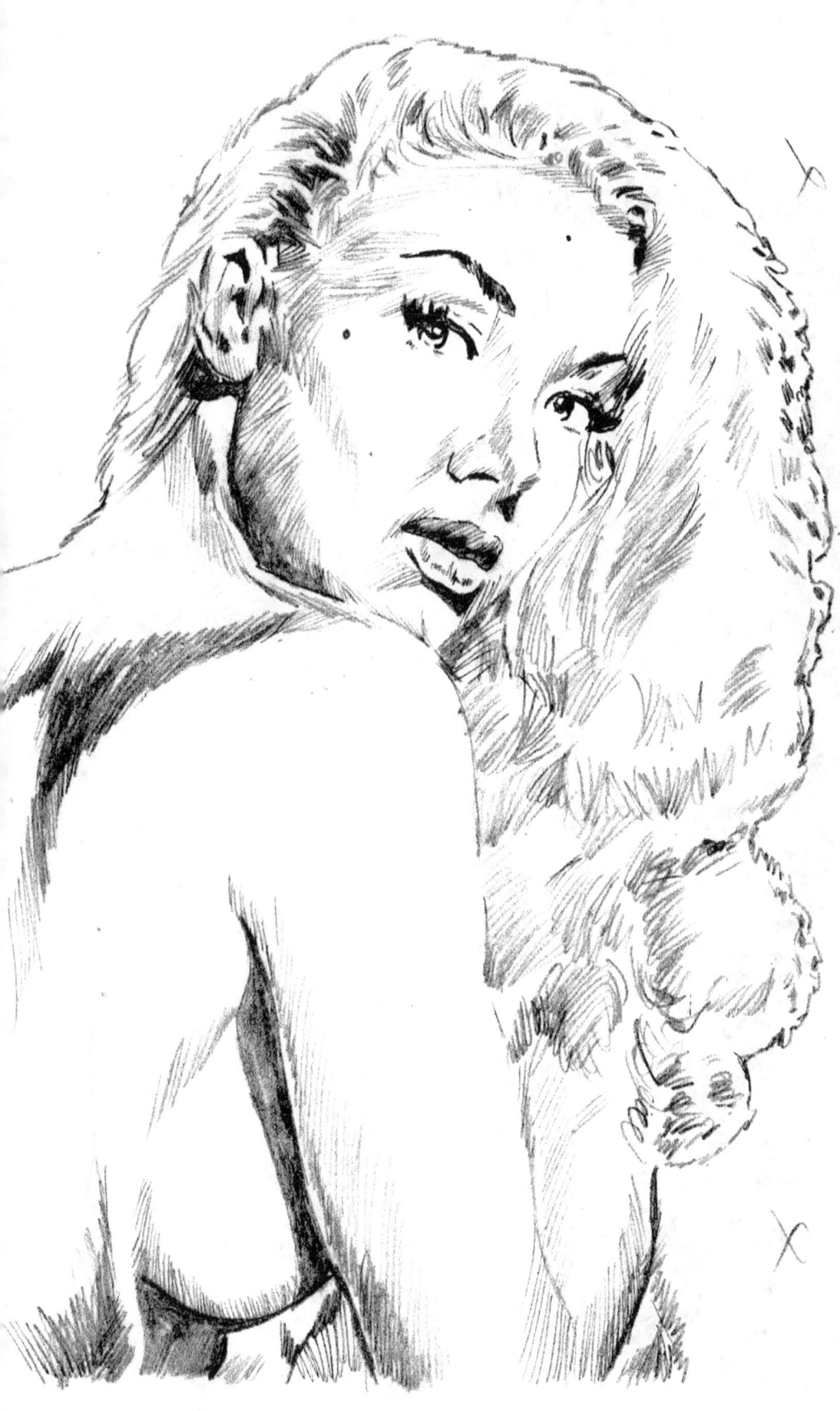

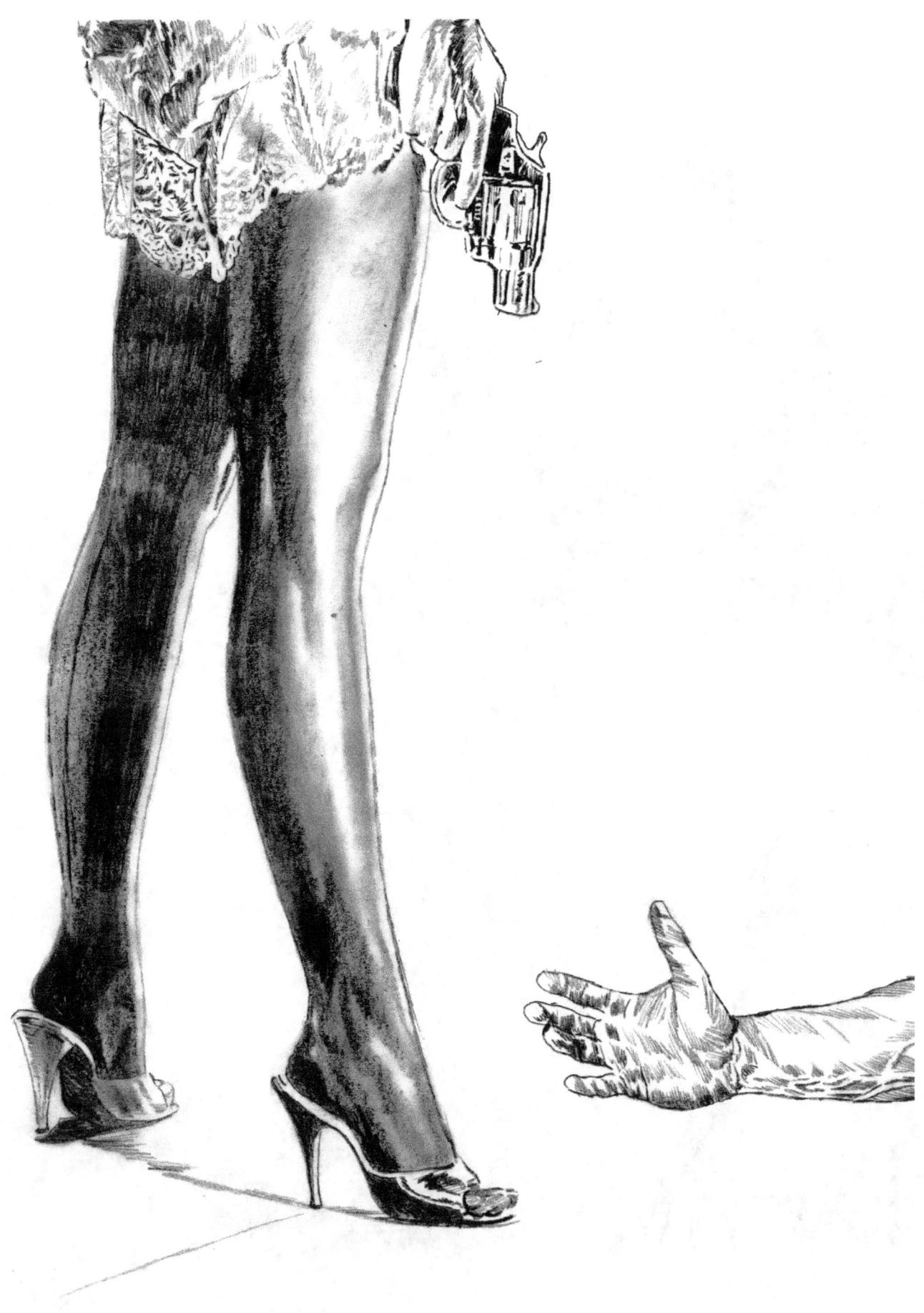

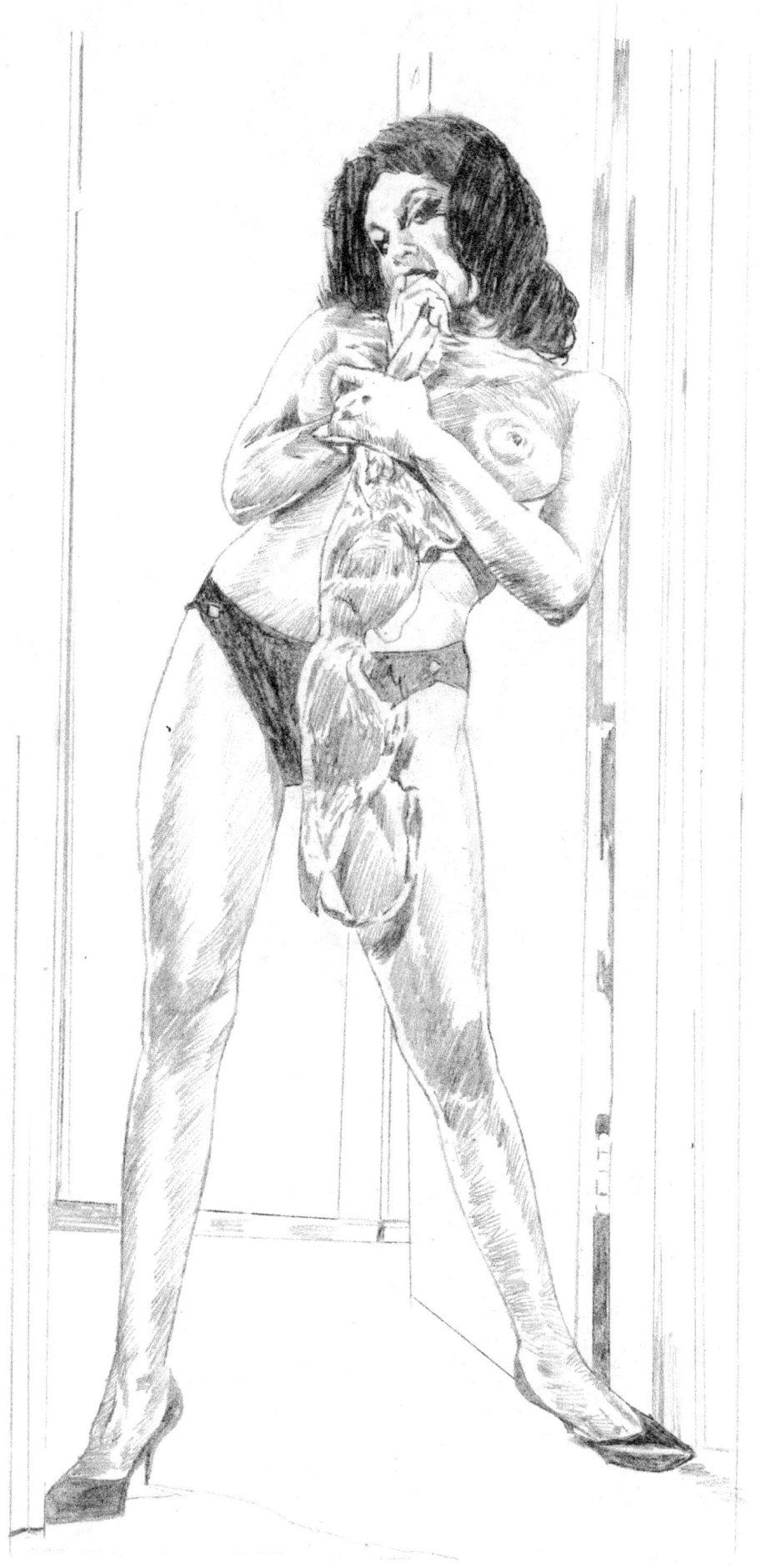

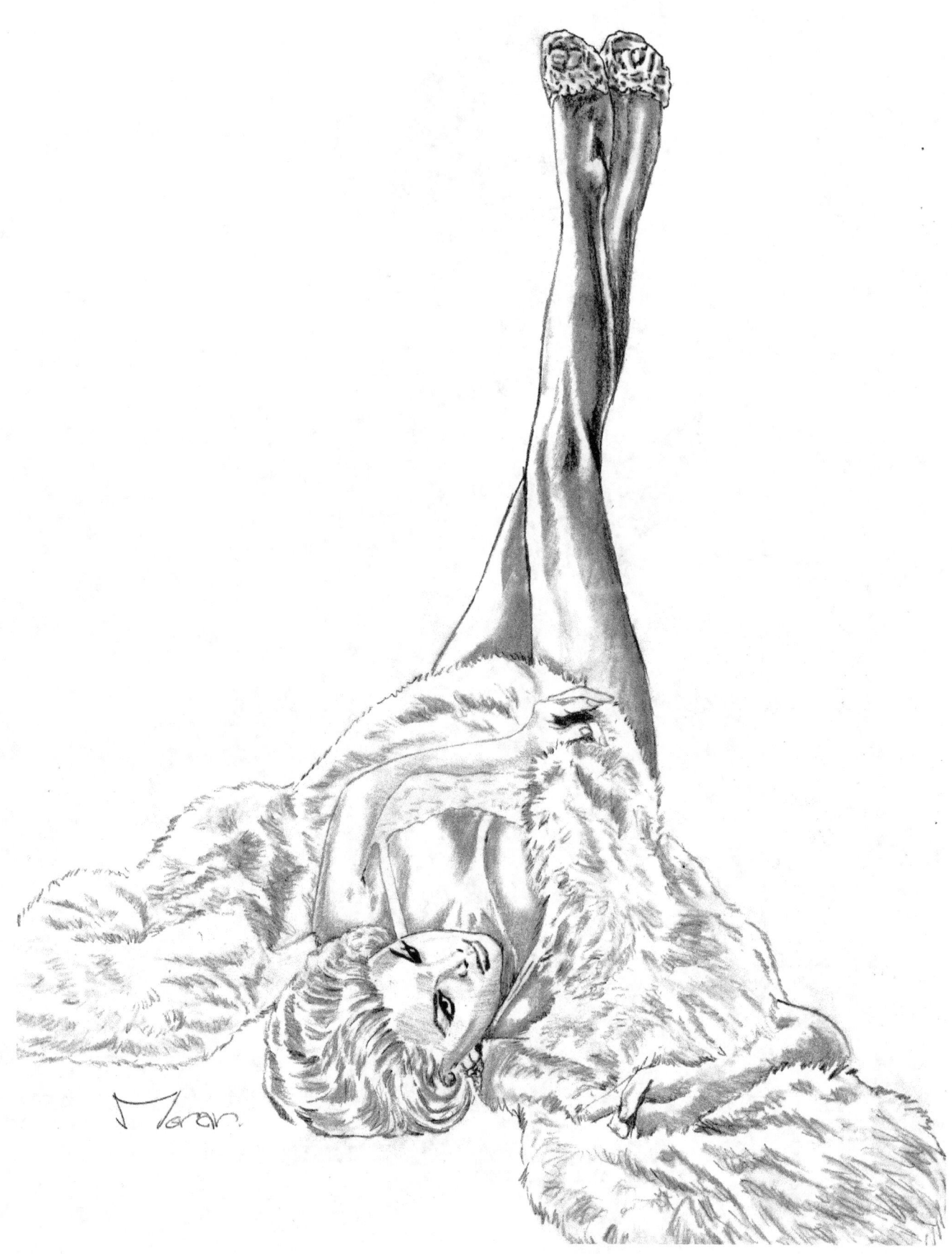

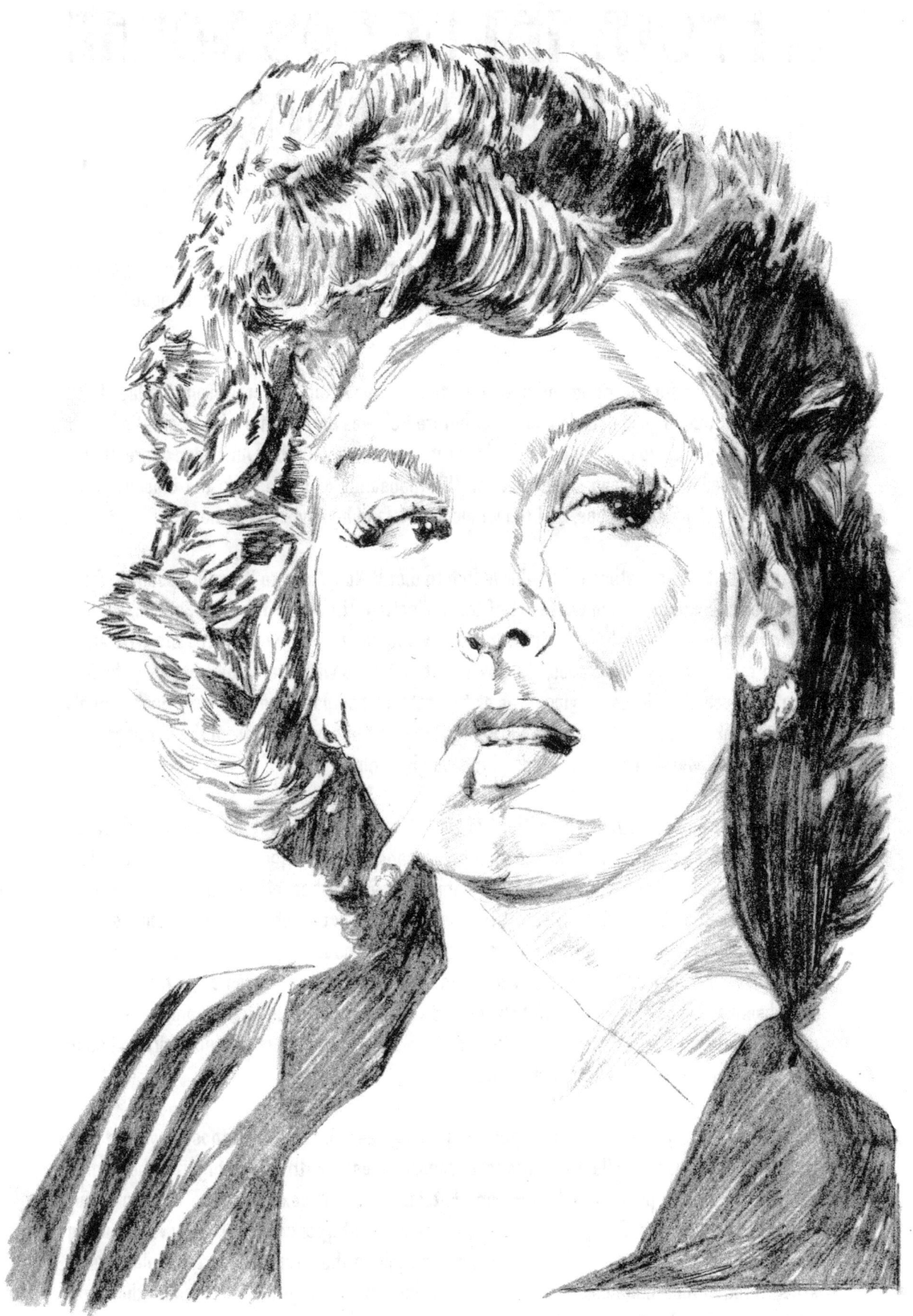

THE NOIR ART OF ROB MORAN – AN AFTERWORD

by Jasper Bark

Sometimes you need a bit of distance to really understand your subject. That distance can be in time or over space. In this stunning collection of Noir art from Rob Moran it happens to be both.

The classic period for the films and literature that we now call 'Noir' ran from the late 1930 to the early 1950s, a good decade and a half before Rob was born. While a lot of great of great Noir has been produced in other countries, Noir is essentially an urban American genre. It was born and raised on the mean streets of the US, thousands of miles from the Glasgow back streets where Rob came of age, and the windswept island he now calls home.

Nonetheless, it's this distance that allows Rob to distill Noir down to its quintessential form in the breathtaking black and white art of this collection. The languid Femme Fatales, holding smoking pistols as casually as a cigarette, the wisecracking PI's whose lives are written in every furrow of their craggy faces, the psychopathic killers with stares devoid of any feeling except malevolence, all seem as iconic as a story by Jim Thompson or a quip from Bogart. Rob's ability to evoke this genre with such clarity and iconic intimacy comes from the distance that an ocean, and several decades of hindsight, have given him.

I've heard it said the attraction of 'Noir' is that it comes from a simpler age, a time when men weren't 'metrosexual' and women didn't worry about being objectified if they wore a low cut dress. However, I think this view is too simplistic and rather misses the point. Noir was a fictional reaction to a turbulent age. A time when all the established economic and societal certainties were being overturned. The great depression robbed men of their position as the sole breadwinner and WWII sent many of them overseas leaving the women to run things in their absence. The savagery that kept the men alive when fighting in Europe, and later Korea, was curtailed by the social niceties of the suburbs where they were supposed to grow old and fat if they were lucky enough to make it home.

Society was dealing with a lot of ambiguity regarding class and gender in those days and Noir was one of the ways the collective national unconscious dealt with this ambiguity. The women in Noir are far from powerless. The Femme Fatales use their sexuality as a weapon of far greater power than the .38 caliber pistols their male counterparts pack. If they're not using their sexuality, the women often have financial muscle, either from money they inherited or earned through their business skills. More often than not they are the ones calling the shots and manipulating the men around them.

66

At the centre of every Noir is a crime, an incident involving certain individuals who break the norms and taboos of society and delve into thoroughly ambiguous areas of human behaviour. The policemen and private dicks charged with investigating these crimes are usually men whose professional and middle class status gives them an entry into an elite circle in which they'll never really be at home due to their blue collar origins. The social status is tested by the ambiguity of the crime and the cracks in the social fabric that it creates.

Even more than cynicism and disenchantment, ambiguity lies at the blackened heart of all Noir. Ambiguity is also at the heart of Rob's art. It's the undepicted grey area that lies between the stark black and white of of these pictures. His women are voluptuous and often in peril, the men step up to protect them, but we are in no doubt as to who really holds the power. The men are full of machismo in the swaggering poses they strike, but behind their eyes lies uncertainty and vulnerability. The phallic pistols they wield are rarely pointed at anything definite, their explosive power is dissipated by the lack of a target, suggesting a subtle emasculation.

I believe it is this ambiguity that makes the book you're holding the finest single collection of Noir art available today. The fallen knights and sultry sirens you'll find in these pages mark Rob out as one of the finest living graphic artists in Europe.

Ladies and Gentlemen, dames and douchebags, I give you the Noir Art of the inestimable Rob Moran.

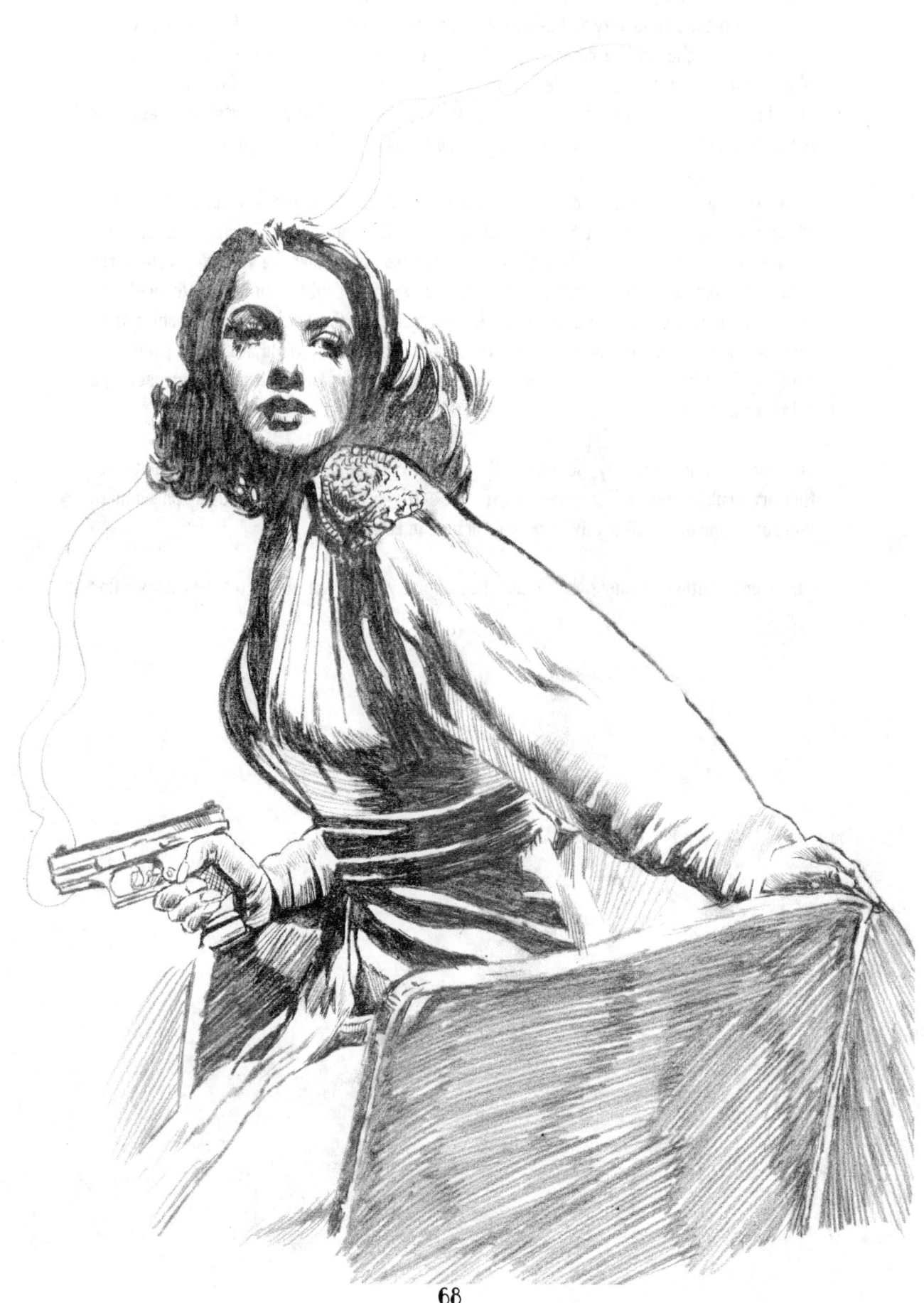

Illustration Index

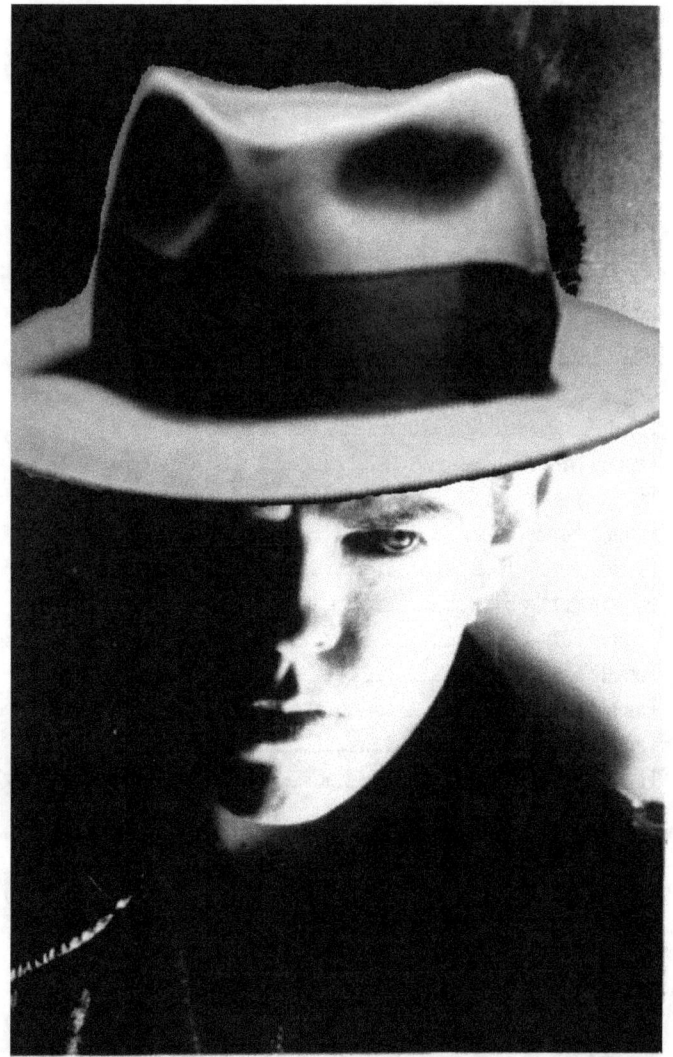

ROB MORAN is an award-winning illustrator/comic book artist/writer based in the UK: as a writer he has created comic book series and written a nationally syndicated American newspaper comic strip. As an artist he has been a magazine illustrator, newspaper cartoonist, computer game designer and created posters for Scottish Opera. As a comic book artist he has worked for publishers in the UK, Europe and the USA such as Marvel, Dark Horse, Image Comics, Silver Phoenix Entertainment, Classical Comics, 2000 AD and many others. His comic book mini-series *BLOOD NATION* is currently being made into a major motion picture. For Airship 27 Productions Rob's work can be found in *Ron Fortier's Brother Bones: Six Days of the Dragon* and *Prohibition*. You can see more of his work at http://robmorancomicart.blogspot.co.uk/

www.ingramcontent.com/pod-product-compliance
Lightning Source LLC
Chambersburg PA
CBHW080822170526
45158CB00009B/2504